EXPERIENCING Jesus
HIS STORY

by

Mark Link, S.J.

Argus Communications
A Division of **DLM**, Inc.
Allen, Texas 75002

Scripture quotations are from the <u>Good</u> <u>News</u> <u>Bible</u>, the Bible in Today's English Version: Copyright © American Bible Society, 1976. Reprinted by permission.

Copyright © 1984 Argus Communications

International Standard Book Number: 0–89505–186–9

Library of Congress Catalog Card Number: 83–73392

Argus Communications
A Division of **DLM,** Inc.
One DLM Park
Allen, Texas 75002

0 9 8 7 6 5 4 3 2 1

Publisher's Note

For two reasons we are delighted to publish this video cassette script of *Experiencing Jesus: His Story*. First, readers can now be served. Second, viewers can be served better. They now have a permanent and handy follow-up resource for deepening their video experience.

The Meditation/Discussion Points following each chapter will help to facilitate personal reflection and group discussion. Except for rare instances, the text transcribes the video script faithfully.

Contents

Jesus

Jesus' Preministry

Jesus' Galilean Ministry

Jesus' Jerusalem Ministry

"I stand at the door and knock; if anyone hears my voice and opens the door, I will come into his house and eat with him, and he will eat with me." *Revelation 3:20*

1. REALITY OF JESUS

Every morning, before starting my work day, I follow the same routine. My friends sometimes kid me about it. But that's okay. After eating breakfast and scanning the lead stories in the morning paper, I go for a walk. Sometimes, as I walk along, I play a game with myself. I ask myself which would be the lead stories, not of just the day, or the year, but of all time. What would be some of your choices? Some of my choices would probably be the discovery of fire, the discovery of America, and the moon landing.

Another one of my choices would be the crucifixion of Jesus. But I don't think most people in the time of Jesus would have regarded it as being very important. They would have seen it as just another Roman execution in some tiny province of the sprawling Roman Empire.

Why the Jesus Story?

One journalist suggested that if news coverage had been as widespread in the time of Jesus as it is today, the story of the death of Jesus might have gotten only a mention in the morning news. It might have gone something like this: "Yesterday, Jesus of Nazareth was executed outside the walls of Jerusalem. Death came at three o'clock Jerusalem time. A violent thunderstorm erupted just after the execution, serving as a fitting climax to the brief but stormy career of the controversial preacher from Galilee. A police guard was posted at the grave site as a precautionary measure."

What makes the crucifixion important, as you know, is not the event itself. In itself, the crucifixion seemed like an end. But an event took place three days after it that changed it from an end to a beginning. And that event comes to mind often as I walk along—especially on those beautiful mornings when the sky is clear, and the sun rises gloriously and triumphantly from the horizon just as Jesus must have risen gloriously and triumphantly from the tomb on that first Easter Sunday.

The sunrise is a beautiful symbol of the resurrection, and rightly so. It drives out the darkness of night and brings in the brightness of day. And that's exactly what the resurrection did. It drove out the darkness of Good Friday and replaced it with the brightness of Easter Sunday.

The Gospel Story

The events of Good Friday left Jesus' followers in a state of shock. Their dream that Jesus had been sent by God to bring about a better world had ended in tragedy. But three days later what seemed to be defeat actually turned into victory. Jesus' followers ran through the streets, shouting the good news: "Jesus is risen! Can you imagine? Jesus is risen!"

This incredible news caught all Jerusalem by surprise, especially the city's authorities. At first, they dismissed the claim as the wishful thinking of Galilean fishermen. But when it became clear that the situation was serious, the authorities called the apostles of Jesus before the Jewish Council and ordered them to stop talking about Jesus in public. But the apostles were filled with the spirit of Pentecost. They refused to keep silent. "We must obey God, not men," they said. When the authorities heard this, they were furious.

But Gamaliel, one of their respected leaders, stood up. He quieted the others down and ordered the apostles to be taken outside. Then he addressed the council. Let's listen to what he says in Acts 5:

"Fellow Israelites, be careful. . . . I tell you, do not take any action against these men. Leave them alone! If what they have planned and done is of human origin, it will disappear, but if it comes from God, you cannot possibly defeat them. You could find yourselves fighting against God!"

(Acts 5:35, 38–39)

Let History Decide

The group took Gamaliel's advice. They agreed with his reasoning. They decided to "let history be the judge" as to whether the Christian movement was of human origin or from God.

So, let's take Gamaliel's advice, also. Let's lay aside the Bible, temporarily, and pick up this history book. Let's see how history is passing judgment on whether the Christian movement was of human origin or from God.

One document in this book was written by a Roman named Tacitus. He wrote it not too long after the Gospel according to John was written. Let me give you some background to the document.

During the reign of Emperor Nero, about 30 years after Gamaliel suggested letting "history be the judge," a great fire broke out in Rome. Rumors spread that Nero himself ordered the fire. He wanted to destroy the old city of Rome, build a new city, and name it for himself. After a week of burning, the fire was finally brought under control. But, then, another fire broke out. Now, rumors spread faster than the flames that Nero, indeed, was behind the fire.

Tacitus

In the weeks that followed, Nero did his best to stop the rumors. But the rumors kept spreading. Finally Nero decided on a desperate move. He tried to shift attention from himself by finding a scapegoat. For his scapegoat he chose a growing religious sect in Rome, called Christians.

Now let's read what Tacitus has to say. He writes: "The sect took its name from Christ, who was put to death during the reign of Emperor Tiberius by sentence of Pontius Pilate. First, known members of the sect were seized. Next, upon their information, crowds were seized. Unusual brutality marked their execution. Some were dressed in wild animal skins and torn to pieces by enraged dogs. Others were put on crosses and, at night, set ablaze to light the darkness."

When you think of this incredible brutality, you cannot help but admire the faith and courage of these early Christians. Sometimes I wonder what I would have done had I been in their shoes.

Pliny

Let me now turn to a second document in this book that sheds light on how history is passing judgment on whether the Christian movement is of human origin or of God. It was written by another Roman, named Pliny the Younger. He wrote about the same time as Tacitus.

Pliny was an official in a Roman province several hundred miles to the east of Rome. The province was having all kinds of problems. The Emperor Trajan asked him who was to blame and what he was doing about the situation. Pliny put the blame on a group called Christians. He said he was dealing with the problem by arresting the Christians and putting pressure on them. He writes: "Those who denied being Christian, I released after they reverenced our gods, honored your image, and defamed Christ. Some admitted they had once been Christian, but no longer were. . . . They admitted gathering regularly at sunrise on a stated day . . . to pray to Christ as to a God. They admitted taking an oath, not for evil intent, but to keep from fraud, theft, adultery, or betraying a trust. After their sunrise meeting, they broke up. But they regathered the same day to share in a harmless meal."

This report on the activity and growth of the early Christian movement is remarkable for four reasons. First, Pliny says the Christians met regularly on a stated day. This is a clear reference to what we now call the Lord's Day.

Second, Pliny says the Christians share a harmless meal. This is a clear reference to what we call the Lord's Supper.

Third, he says Christians pray to Christ as to a God. This is a clear reference to what we call the Lord's divinity.

Fourth, Pliny says Christians take an oath not to betray a trust and so forth. This is a clear reference to the Lord's style or way of life that he taught his followers.

Isn't it remarkable to find such a clear statement of the basic creed, code, and cult of Christianity correctly described by a very early Roman historian? By creed, we mean what Christians believed. By code, we mean how Christians lived out their belief in daily life. By cult, we mean how Christians worshipped together as a community. Pliny ends his letter to the Emperor saying: "I now want your advice on this matter, because the number of Christians is growing. But I am confident we can contain them."

The Christian movement was not stopped: Today Christianity not only survives, it continues to grow and to spread throughout the world. Jesus and his teaching continue to excite us; they continue to inspire us, to stir our hearts and our imaginations. And two thousand years after the resurrection, the impact of Jesus on history continues to grow also.

History: Jesus Stands First

One modern historian, H. G. Wells, was asked to pick the top six people in the history of the world. He placed Jesus first. Wells pointed out that his choice was not influenced by the fact that many people believe Jesus to be the Son of God. "I am speaking of Jesus as a man. . . . The historian must treat him as a man just as a painter must paint him as a man. . . . He must adhere to evidence that would pass unchallenged if his book were to be read in every nation under the sun. That place is his by virtue of the profound ideas which he released."

Fatherhood of God

The test of a person's greatness, says Wells, is what did he leave to grow? What ideas or seeds did he plant that still continue to grow and bear fruit. By this test, Wells says, Jesus stands first.

What were some of the profound ideas or seeds, if you will, that Jesus left to grow? Wells singles out two in particular. The first is the notion of the fatherhood of God. It is the notion that the creator of this vast universe cares, really cares about us, you and me. Because we have God as our father we are all brothers and sisters, one family. If we ever really begin living out this reality, says Wells, it will change the world. It makes you ask: Why is it that we don't live out this reality more faithfully than we do?

Kingdom of God

The second idea or seed that Jesus left to grow, according to Wells, is the "Kingdom of God"; it is the idea that all human beings have destiny. Human history is going somewhere; it has a direction. God has a plan, and all of us have a part to play in it.

I'd like to digress for a minute, here, to tell you a personal story. It illustrates the point that everyone has a part to play in God's plan and that no part is too small to count. Years ago I was teaching at a high school in Detroit. One morning I picked up the newspaper and noticed a story on the front page. It was about a man who owned a summer home on Lake Erie.

One Friday night he drove to the home to get it ready for the summer season. In the middle of the night he was awakened by a fire that had spread from the fireplace. Since his phone was not in operation, he drove to a pay phone on the expressway. When he got there he plunged his hands into his pockets for a coin. Would you believe, he didn't have a single coin to his name. All he had was a wallet full of bills. At that moment, he would have given every bill in his wallet, and a hundred more, for one thin dime.

I like that story, because, if you're like me, there are times when you feel small and insignificant. You feel, literally, as worthless as a dime. But God's ways are not our ways. And who knows, in God's plan we may be more important than a wallet full of hundred dollar bills. As a matter of fact, scripture shows over and over again that God often chose little people, the "dimes" of life, to do some of his biggest jobs.

Take Gideon. The Bible says he came from the most insignificant clan in all Israel. Yet God chose him to lead Israel against its enemy. Take David, also. The Bible says he was the least eligible of Jesse's eight sons. Yet God chose him to be Israel's king. Paul says this about God's choice of "little people" to do some of his biggest jobs:

God purposely chose what the world considers nonsense in order to shame the wise, and he chose what the world considers weak in order to shame the powerful.

(1 Corinthians 1:27)

Jesus Changes People

Two thousand years after the resurrection of Jesus, history shows that Christianity not only survives, it continues to grow. And the impact of Jesus on history continues to grow also.

Let's now move away from what the Bible says about Jesus and what history says about Jesus to what people today say about him. For me, personally, one of the most dramatic testimonies of what people today say is found in this book, *Through the Valley of the Kwai,* by Ernest Gordon. This is a true story that took place along the Kwai Noi River, in Thailand, during World War II. It has since been immortalized in the film *The Bridge Over the River Kwai.*

Along the banks of this river, 12,000 prisoners of war died of disease, starvation, and brutality while building a railroad. Working in heat that sometimes soared to 120 degrees, husky men became walking skeletons in weeks. Morale in the camp dipped to zero. Something had to be done. Two prisoners organized Bible study groups. The result was beyond belief.

He writes: "Through their readings and discussions the prisoners came to know Jesus as a real person. Jesus was one of us. Like us, he often had no place to lay his head. No food for his belly, no friends in high places. He, too, had known bone-weariness from too much toil." Everything about Jesus—what he was, what he said, what he did—began to make sense to them. With this new understanding Jesus' crucifixion became very real and very meaningful. It told them that Jesus was in their midst, suffering with them.

"They stopped thinking about themselves as victims of some tragic situation. They began to see that suffering comes not from God, but from human viciousness and stupidity."

In a beautiful passage, Gordon writes: "Nowhere was the change in attitude more manifest than in our prayers. We learned to pray for others more than for ourselves. When we did pray for ourselves, it was not to get something, but to release some power within us."

One night when Gordon was hobbling back to his shack after a late meeting, he heard the sound of men singing. Someone was keeping time with a stick on a piece of tin. The sound of the singing and the sound of the stick hitting the tin made the darkness come alive. The difference between that joyful sound and the deathly silence of months back, says Gordon, "was the difference between life and death."

Years ago, I was in England giving a retreat to some men. During one of the talks, I told this same story. Afterward, a man came up to me and said: "Father, I presume you will tell that story again. When you do, tell your listeners that it was even more remarkable than the way you describe it. I should know. I was there."

And so, Jesus is not only someone who continues to influence history in a powerful way, but also someone who continues to influence people in a powerful way. And it is through those people even though they may seem to be insignificant, that Jesus continues to build up his kingdom on earth.

Five Jesuses

Let me share with you another story that shows how Jesus can change our lives—your life and mine—if we just have the courage to open our hearts to him. The story appeared years ago in *Guideposts* magazine. It was called "The Five Christs I Have Known" by Leonard LeSourd.

LeSourd was having dinner one night with ten other people. They were discussing a movie about Jesus. Suddenly, a young woman, bored with the conversation, said, "Well who would want to be like Jesus anyway?" A deafening silence followed.

Then someone changed the subject and the conversation continued. Afterward, LeSourd asked himself this question: "Why did the girl's remark produce such a negative reaction?" How would you respond to this question?

Here's LeSourd's answer to his own question. Perhaps some of the guests were intimidated by her remark. Maybe some were as bored as she was. And still others may not have known Jesus well enough to decide whether they wanted to be like him or not. Then LeSourd asked himself about his own understanding of Jesus. After a great deal of thought, he concluded that he had known "Five Christs" in his life.

Fanciful Jesus

His first knowledge of Jesus came by way of Sunday school class, when he was nine years old. Specifically, it came from a picture of a pale, anemic-faced Christ that hung on the Sunday school wall. This pathetic Christ didn't inspire a boy who was just discovering life, a boy who was having too much fun just trying to figure out who he was to take time off to figure out who Jesus was. And so, LeSourd's first Christ was a "Fanciful Christ" who existed only in his immature mind.

Historical Jesus

LeSourd met his second Christ in college. This was the "Historical Christ" who lived two thousand years ago. It is the Christ who H. G. Wells ranked first in history. This Christ impressed LeSourd but had no real personal impact upon his life. The "Historical Christ" was just a good person, like Lincoln or Washington.

Jesus the Teacher

LeSourd met his third Christ after he came out of military service. He had the leisure to do whatever he wanted. He toured the United States and gathered data for what was to be his "Great American Novel." But, eventually, LeSourd ran out of money. Fortunately, he was lucky enough to land a job with a new Christian magazine. His first assignment was to interview people about their faith. He was surprised to learn that many very successful people really lived their lives according to the teaching of Jesus. Now he really wanted to know more about Jesus. This man was a simple Galilean peasant, but the giants of history depended upon him for guidance.

Jesus My Savior

LeSourd met his fourth Christ while on retreat with some young friends. The theme of this retreat was commitment to Jesus. It was a beautiful experience of prayer and sharing. During the retreat, one of the young men told the group of the joy he felt after he had gone into the chapel, knelt down, and committed his life to Jesus. LeSourd was embarrassed by his openness. But he found himself wanting what the young man had found. Just before the retreat ended, LeSourd went into the chapel, knelt down, and made his own personal commitment to Jesus. From that day on Jesus became the center of his life.

Indwelling Jesus

LeSourd's introduction to his fifth and final Christ came about in an unexpected way. Years after the retreat he found himself being tempted to do something that no Christian should ever do. It was a kind of major temptation we all go through at one time or another. He felt himself falling, and he reached out, frantically, for something to hold on to. He found it in the commitment he had made years before on the retreat. "Thus," says LeSourd, "I began my fifth and most meaningful relationship with Jesus—my contact with the Holy Spirit, the Indwelling Christ." It was contact with the life-giving spirit of the risen Christ.

Everything began to fit together. LeSourd now understood how the Apostles had committed their lives to Jesus, too. But when severe temptation came to them, just as it came to him, they also fell back in their old ways. Judas betrayed Jesus, Peter denied Jesus, and the rest fled. It wasn't until Pentecost when they received the Holy Spirit of Jesus that the Apostles really changed. On that important day in the history of the church the spirit of the risen Jesus began to "indwell" the followers of Jesus in a powerful new way.

We might liken LeSourd's gradual growth in his understanding of Christ—over five stages—to the growth of a plant over five stages. The first Christ, the "Fanciful Christ," would correspond to the seed of the plant. The second Christ, the "Historical Christ," would correspond to the green stem that emerges from the seed. The third Christ, the "Teacher Christ," would correspond to the bud that eventually forms at the top of the stem. The fourth Christ, the "Savior Christ," would correspond to the flower that bursts from the bud. And the fifth Christ, the "Indwelling Christ," would correspond to the fruit that develops from the flower of the plant.

Who Do You Say I Am?

As you think about each of these five stages, you might ask yourself how LeSourd's experience of Jesus corresponds to your own experience of Jesus. How do you experience Jesus in your own personal life—right now? The Bible says Jesus is risen. Recall Gamaliel and his proposal to the authorities about the movement of Jesus. History says Jesus was the greatest man that ever lived. Recall H. G. Wells and his evaluation of Jesus. And we have just seen the powerful effect that Jesus still has on the lives of people like the prisoners of war along the Kwai Noi River and LeSourd.

But the important thing, here and now in your life, right now, is not what the Bible says, nor what history says, nor what other people say. The important thing is what you say. How do you experience Jesus in your life, right now?

Put yourself in this gospel scene and answer the question Jesus asks:

One day, when Jesus was praying alone, the disciples came to him. "Who do the crowds say I am?" he asked them.

"Some say that you are John the Baptist," they answered. "Others say that you are Elijah, while others say that one of the prophets of long ago has come back to life."

"What about you?" he asked them. "Who do you say I am?"

(Luke 9:18-20)

MEDITATION/DISCUSSION POINTS

1. "Jesus' followers ran through the streets shouting the good news: 'Jesus is risen! Can you imagine? Jesus is risen!' " What convinces you most that Jesus is risen, as the gospel says?

2. Gamaliel told his colleagues: "Do not take action against these men. . . . If what they have planned and done is of human origin it will disappear, but if it comes from God, you cannot possibly defeat them." What convinces you most that the Christian movement is from God?

3. The Roman historian Tacitus says of the Roman Christians: "Some were . . . torn to pieces by enraged dogs. Others were . . . set ablaze to light the darkness." Recall a time when you were put down or suffered for something you believed to be right.

4. Leonard LeSourd said his relationship with Jesus passed through five stages. How has your own relationship with Jesus passed through stages or changed over the years?

5. Jesus asked his disciples, "Who do you say I am?" Do you find this question hard or easy to answer? Why?

Now, there are many other things that Jesus did. If they were all written down one by one, I suppose that the whole world could not hold the books that would be written. *John 21:25*

2. BOOKS OF JESUS

Let's do a little science-fiction dreaming. Suppose a modern camera crew got into the time machine and flew backward into history 2,000 years to the time of Jesus. Suppose they were able to film the entire life of Jesus, from his birth in Bethlehem on Christmas to his resurrection.

Think of it! You could enter the world of Jesus, exactly as it was. You would see the very people Jesus saw as he walked about. And you would see Jesus, exactly as he was. You would actually see him place his hands on the blind beggar and bring back his sight.

Would You Trade?

Let us suppose, further, that technicians fed the film into a computer and programmed it. By merely typing the name of any event in the life of Jesus, you could make the event appear on the screen in full sound and color, just the way it actually took place. Now suppose you were given a choice. You could have either the printed gospels or computerized access to the film of the complete life of Jesus. Would you be willing to make such a trade—the printed gospels for the computerized film? Remember! You would have to give up the printed gospels entirely.

Further, suppose that you would have to choose not only for yourself but for everyone else, too. In other words, if you chose the film, future generations of Christians would no longer have the four printed gospels. Instead, they would have only a film of the actual life of Jesus. This means that they would actually see and hear Jesus exactly as people in his time saw and heard him. Would you make that trade?

I often ask young people this question before starting a scripture course with them. Their responses are always interesting.

What My Students Said

For example, some say the film would be too long. Thirty-three years? You'd never be able to view it completely. People would have to rely on condensed versions of it. Editors of an abridged version could slant it to fit their own personal viewpoint of Jesus. Others say the film would be in a language that is no longer widely used. Even biblical experts would have trouble understanding it. Still others say a film would be fantastic. They point out that there would be no more arguments about whether Jesus did or did not walk on water, and so forth.

Why the Gospels?

After the students discuss the question thoroughly, I find that they divide about evenly on whether they would make the trade or not. Invariably they ask me, "What would you do?" I tell them that I would stay with the printed gospels as they appear in the Bible. Why? Because even the disciples of Jesus did not always understand everything that Jesus said or did.

Take the time when Jesus drove the money changers out of the temple. John says of this event:

The Jewish authorities came back to him with a question, "What miracle can you perform to show us that you have the right to do this?" Jesus answered, "Tear down this temple, and in three days I will build it up again." "Are you going to build it again in three days?" they asked him. "It has taken forty-six years to build this temple!" But the temple Jesus was speaking about was his body. So when he was raised from death, his disciples remembered that he had said this, and they believed the scripture and what Jesus had said.

(John 2:18-22)

Take also Palm Sunday. On that unforgettable day the disciples of Jesus cut branches from trees and went out to meet Jesus. He was entering the city riding on a donkey, as the prophets had foretold. But the disciples got so carried away in the excitement that the significance of the event went right over their heads. After describing the Palm Sunday event, John says:

The disciples of Jesus did not understand this at the time. But when Jesus had been raised to glory, they remembered that the scripture said this about him and that they had done this for him.

(John 12:16)

Light from the Spirit

What happened after Jesus had been raised that caused his disciples to understand the Palm Sunday event? Exactly what Jesus said would happen. On Pentecost, the Holy Spirit came down upon the followers of Jesus and transformed them in a remarkable way. And that's what Jesus said would happen.

"When I go, you will not be left all alone. . . . The helper, the Holy Spirit, whom the Father will send in my name, will teach you everything and make you remember all that I have told you."

(John 14:18, 26)

That's just what happened on Pentecost. After the Holy Spirit came, all the events in the life of Jesus and all his teachings came together in an unbelievable way. It was as though the Holy Spirit gave the disciples new eyes to see with and a new mind to understand with.

For this reason the printed gospels in the Bible are more valuable than a computerized film of everything Jesus ever said or did. If we had only a film view, we would most certainly miss the deeper meaning of many things Jesus said and did, just as his disciples did. We would not grasp the significance of what was happening. An example might help.

Roger Price wrote a very entertaining book years ago. He called it *Droodles*. A droodle is something like a doodle. A doodle, as you know, is something you draw when you are talking on the telephone or listening to someone talk at a meeting. You pick up a pencil and start to draw meaningless little objects and shapes. A droodle is kind of like that. A droodle is a drawing that seems to be absolutely meaningless until it is given its proper title. Let me illustrate by drawing for you one of the droodles from Price's book.

Do you have any ideas about what it is?

Price entitles it, "A man in a tuxedo who stood too close to the elevator doors."

Here's another droodle. Can you guess what it is?

Price entitles it, "A fat man smoking a pipe in a soft bed."

And here's a final one for you, created by one of my students.

That's a little boy with too many balloons.

Birthday of the Gospels

Many events in the life of Jesus were like droodles. That is, they didn't make sense until the Holy Spirit gave them their title, so to speak, on Pentecost. Pentecost could be called the "birthday" of the gospel.

Maybe I can give you another example that will dramatize even better the difference Pentecost made in the disciples' understanding of the life and teaching of Jesus. I'm sure you have seen the familiar camera commercial on television. Two people are talking. Suddenly someone appears with a camera and takes a picture. And, lo and behold, out of the camera rolls an apparently blank sheet of paper. Nothing seems to be on it. But then, miracle of miracles, before your very eyes, shapes and colors start to appear. As if by magic, the blank paper comes alive.

The events of the life of Jesus were something like that. They revealed their full meaning only gradually. Jesus had said during his lifetime, "I have much more to tell you, but now it would be too much for you to bear. When, however, the Spirit comes . . . he will lead you into all truth."

And so, at first, as far as meaning was concerned, some events in the life of Jesus appeared to be like a blank sheet of paper. There didn't seem to be anything special about them.

But then came Pentecost! All of the sudden, when exposed to the light of Pentecost, all of these events came alive. Their significance or deeper meaning began to emerge in a breathtaking new way. The followers of Jesus were so filled with excitement and energy that they ran out into the streets and began to preach the good news of Jesus. On the first day alone, 3,000 people became believers. The followers of Jesus were filled with a power and excitement that moved and inspired practically everyone who heard them preach.

Why Preached First?

And so on Pentecost, the gospels in this Bible were born. The difference in the disciples' understanding of the teaching of Jesus before Pentecost and after it was as striking as the difference in our understanding of a droodle before it gets its title and after it gets it, or the difference in a film immediately after it rolls out of a camera and a few minutes later, when it has been exposed to the light. The reaction of the followers of Jesus to Pentecost was not to pick up a pen and write out their exciting new vision of the life and teaching of Jesus. It never occurred to them to do this. Their reaction was to run out into the streets of Jerusalem and share the "good news" with everyone who would listen.

One reason why it never occurred to the followers of Jesus to write down the good news of Jesus was because they saw no need to do so. They believed Jesus would return soon. Recall what took place immediately after the ascension of Jesus.

> *Jesus was taken up to heaven as they watched him, and a cloud hid him from their sight. They still had their eyes fixed on the sky as he went away, when two men in white suddenly stood beside them and said, "Galileans, why are you standing there looking up at the sky? This Jesus, who was taken from you into heaven, will come back in the same way that you saw him go to heaven."*
>
> *(Acts 1:9-11)*

From what is said elsewhere in the gospel, it appears that the disciples of Jesus believed Jesus would return immediately after they had preached the gospel to every nation. The disciples thought they could complete this preaching task in their own lifetime. They saw no need to write down the gospel.

Nothing Stopped Them

For the next twenty or thirty years, the gospel was preached far and wide, in synagogues, over dinner tables, on street corners. With a burning urgency, the apostles carried the good news of Jesus beyond the walls of Jerusalem, eventually to Rome itself. Often they met with fierce opposition, even persecution. Some were hung on crosses, like Jesus their master. Some were ripped apart by beasts in the arena. Others were burned alive. But no amount of opposition or persecution could stop them from preaching the good news.

A few years ago I got a special insight into the kind of dedication and commitment that these early Christians must have had. I ran across a story about an old man who lived in a village in New Guinea. He earned his living by cutting firewood for the ovens of the missionary hospital outside the village. Everybody called the old man "One Tooth," because his upper jaw contained only one tooth.

Because he was Christian and had just learned to read, One Tooth spent a part of every day reading the gospel story to outpatients as they waited for the doctor to treat them. Day after day, week after week, the old woodcutter shared his faith in Jesus with the suffering people who came to the mission hospital for help.

Then something happened. The old man began to have trouble reading. At first, he thought it was something minor, something that would clear up in a day or two. But instead of clearing up, it got much worse. One Tooth went to see the missionary doctor. The doctor looked into his right eye, then into his left eye. "Can you see anything wrong?" One Tooth asked nervously.

The doctor put his arm around One Tooth's shoulder. "Yes," said the doctor. "There is something wrong, seriously wrong, with both your eyes. You are going blind." "Oh no!" said One Tooth. "I'm already old. Now I'll be blind and useless, also."

The next day, One Tooth didn't show up to read the gospel to the outpatients. He had vanished. Later the doctor learned that One Tooth had left the village. He was now living alone in a deserted section of the island. A boy who was supplying the old man with food told the doctor where he was.

So the doctor went to see One Tooth. "What are you doing here?" asked the doctor. "Why didn't you stay at the hospital?"

One Tooth replied, "Doctor, ever since the day that you told me I was going blind, I have been reading and memorizing the most important parts of the Bible. I've memorized the parts about the birth of Jesus, a number of his miracles and parables, his Sermon on the Mount, and his death and resurrection. I've been repeating these parts over and over to the boy, to make sure I've got them right. In about a week, I'll be back at the hospital, Doctor, telling the story of Jesus, again, to the outpatients."

When I finished reading that story, I couldn't help but think that this must have been the kind of commitment and dedication the early Christians had. Nothing could keep them from sharing the good news of Jesus. No obstacle was too great to overcome. The only thing that mattered was telling other people about Jesus.

The Gospels Get Recorded

As the followers of Jesus walked the long distance from village to village and city to city sharing the good news, it became clear to them that they wouldn't be able to preach the gospel to every nation within their lifetime. They wouldn't even come close.

This created a problem. How could they make sure that key portions of the life and teaching of Jesus would not be lost or forgotten after their death? Peter refers to this problem in his second letter. "I shall soon put off this mortal body, as our Lord Jesus Christ plainly told me. I will do my best, then, to provide a way for you to remember these matters at all times after." (2 Peter 1:14-15)

But there was yet another reason why the apostles decided to write down the gospel. It was because some people were beginning to distort the good news. Paul says in Galatians 1, "There are some people who are upsetting you and trying to change the gospel." (Galatians 1:7)

And so, guided by the Holy Spirit, the evangelists began the tedious job of collecting, studying, and ordering the important events and teachings in the life of Jesus. In the introduction to his gospel, Luke describes the process:

And so, your excellency, because I have carefully studied all these matters from their beginning, I thought it would be good to write an orderly account for you. I do this so that you will know the full truth about everything you have been taught."

(Luke 1:3–4)

Gospel Stages

So the gospels were written down, just as they appear in the Bible today. These gospels, then, are the final stage of a three-stage process. The first stage was the actual life of Jesus. That is what the apostles saw with their own eyes and heard with their own ears. John refers to this life stage in his first letter:

We have heard it and we have seen it with our eyes; yes we have seen it, and our hands have touched it. . . . What we have seen and heard we announce to you also, so that you will join with us in a fellowship that we have with the Father and with his Son, Jesus Christ.

(1 John 1:1, 3)

And so the first stage was the life stage. That is, what the disciples saw Jesus do with their own eyes and what they heard him say with their own ears.

Next, there was the word-of-mouth or oral stage, which began on Pentecost day. Guided by the Holy Spirit, the apostles preached by word of mouth, or in an oral way, what they themselves were eyewitnesses to.

Finally, there was the written stage. It began when it became clear to the apostles that they would not be able to preach the good news of Jesus to every nation themselves. And so, guided by the Holy Spirit, they wrote down the good news of Jesus.

Gospel Evidence

Some people ask, "How long did the oral stage last?" In other words, how many years passed from Pentecost to the day the first evangelist put pen to paper? We really don't know. Some say perhaps as many as thirty years. But, again, we just don't know.

Matthew does make two interesting references to the time interval in his gospel. Speaking of Judas, Matthew writes:

> When Judas, the traitor, learned that Jesus had been condemned, he repented and took back the thirty silver coins... Judas threw the coins down in the temple and left; then he went off and hanged himself.
>
> The chief priests picked up the coins and said, "This is blood money, and it is against our law to put it in the temple treasury." After reaching an agreement about it, they used the money to buy Potter's Field as a cemetery for foreigners. That is why that field is called "Field of Blood" to this very day.
>
> (Matthew 27:3, 5-8)

The key words are "to this very day." This clearly indicates that Matthew is writing a considerable length of time after the event actually took place.

Matthew's second reference to the time interval occurs in connection with the resurrection.

> The soldiers guarding the tomb went back to the city and told the chief priests everything that had happened. The chief priests met with the elders and made their plan; they gave a large sum of money to the soldiers and said: "You are to say

that Jesus' disciples came during the night and stole his body while you were asleep. And if the governor should hear of this we will convince him that you are innocent, and you will have nothing to worry about."

The guards took the money and did what they were told to do. And so that is the report spread around by the Jews to this very day.

(Matthew 28:11–15)

The key words, again, are "to this very day." Again, they clearly indicate that Matthew is writing a considerable length of time after the event took place.

Shell Image

A friend of mine has an interesting way of looking at the three stages by which the gospel developed. He compares them to a familiar phenomenon in nature. The ocean floor is covered with thousands upon thousands of sea shells. In time a small percentage of these shells get washed ashore, just as this one did. They lie on the beach. The surf washes them, and the sun softens their color. Then, one day, an artist comes walking along the beach and picks up some of the shells. He takes them home and painstakingly forms them into a lovely vase.

The shells on the ocean floor correspond to the life stage of the gospel, that is, to all those things Jesus said and did during his entire lifetime. John talks about all these things at the end of his gospel:

Now, there are many other things that Jesus did. If they were all written down one by one, I suppose

that the whole world could not hold the books that
would be written.

(John 21:25)

So, the floor shells correspond to the life stage. The shells that get washed up onto the shore correspond to the second stage of the gospel, that is, the oral stage. It began on Pentecost and continued until the first evangelist put pen to paper. Finally, there are the shells that are picked up by the artist and formed into a lovely vase. These vase shells correspond to the written stage.

Three Options

Let's conclude with one final point about the third stage, the written stage. When the evangelists sat down to record their gospels, each found himself in a situation not unlike a television editor who must put together a two-hour special of a world figure who just died. The editor has miles of television footage of all kinds of events from the celebrity's life. He also has footage of scores of speeches that the person gave.

The editor can approach the arrangement of this footage in three different ways. First, he can take a historical approach. He can arrange the footage in the exact order that it was filmed in the person's life. This approach would be purely informational. Second, he can take a biographical approach. He can arrange the footage in a way to show the personal growth and development of the celebrity. This approach would be not only informational but also inspirational. Third, he can take an experiential approach. By that I mean, he can arrange the events in a way that would invite his viewers to experience the celebrity in the same way that people who knew him experienced him. This approach would be not only informational and inspirational but also invitational. That is, it would involve the viewer actively.

Invitation to Faith

The evangelists had the same choice to make when it came to presenting the story of Jesus. Guided by the Holy Spirit, each gospel writer presented the story of Jesus not in the form of a history that informs, not in the form of a biography that inspires, but in the form of a gospel that invites. Each gospel writer presented his story of Jesus as an invitation to readers to try to experience some of the excitement of Jesus that the disciples themselves experienced.

In other words, they wanted to do much more than merely inform their readers about Jesus. They wanted to invite their readers to believe in Jesus. John emphasized this important point when he says of the events in his gospel, "These have been written in order that you may believe that Jesus is the Messiah, the Son of God, and that through faith in him, you may have life."

After reading any of these books on a library shelf, you can say, "Now that was an interesting book," or "I didn't care for that book." We all tend to pass judgment on a book and what it says. With the Bible, it is the opposite. The Bible is not just another book. It is the word of God. We don't pass judgment on the Bible. The Bible passes judgment on us.

Invitation to Life

To put it in another way, the Bible is not a book about life; it is an invitation to life. It is an invitation from God to experience Jesus and to enter into a personal relationship with him. And like every other invitation, the Bible has an R.S.V.P. attached.

How have you responded in the past to God's invitation to experience the love and saving power of Jesus? How are you responding to it now? How would you like to respond to it in the future, beginning right now, at this very moment?

Let me close with one of my favorite readings about Jesus. Its author is unknown. He says of Jesus:

"Here is a young man who was born in a obscure village, the child of a peasant woman. He worked in a carpenter's shop until he was thirty, and then for three years he was an itinerant preacher. He never wrote a book. He never held an office. He never owned a home. He never had a family. He did none of the things we usually associate with greatness. He had no credentials but himself.

"While he was still a young man, the tide of public opinion turned against him. His friends ran away. He was turned over to his enemies. He went through a mockery of a trial. He was nailed to a cross between two thieves. While he was dying, his executioners gambled for the only piece of property he had on earth, and that was his coat. When he was dead he was laid in a borrowed tomb through the pity of a friend.

"Nineteen centuries have come and gone, and today he is the central figure of the human race, and the leader of progress. All the armies that ever marched, all the navies that ever sailed, all the parliaments that ever sat, all the kings that ever reigned put together, have not affected the life of man upon this earth as has this one solitary life."

MEDITATION/DISCUSSION POINTS

1. If you could take a time machine back to Jesus' time and witness one of the following events, which would you pick and why: Jesus' birth, the Last Supper, the crucifixion, the resurrection?

2. The book says: "At first . . . some events in the life of Jesus appeared to be like a blank sheet of paper. There didn't seem to be anything special about them." Why is it harder or easier to believe in modern times than it was in gospel times?

3. Why don't more Christians today work as hard as One Tooth did to share their faith in Jesus with other people?

4. The book says, "[The Bible] is an invitation from God to experience Jesus and to enter into a personal relationship with him." How can you experience Jesus, and how can you develop a relationship with him?

5. The book asks, "How have you responded in the past to God's invitation to experience the love and saving power of Jesus? How are you responding to it now? How would you like to respond to it in the future, beginning right now?" Answer each question, using examples to illustrate.

"I am the light of the world. . . . Whoever follows me will have the light of life. . . ." *John 8:12*

3. PORTRAITS OF JESUS

I don't know how familiar you are with Chicago, but a visitor can approach the city four different ways: the way boats approach it, across choppy, cold, waters; the way cars approach it, along one of the many ribbons of concrete that flow into the city from every direction; the way an Amtrack train approaches it, along a pair of fragile, shiny rails; or the way planes overhead approach it. And if you've ever flown into Chicago on a clear night, you know what a spectacular sight it is. Each approach to Chicago, whether it be by road or by rail, by air or by water, gives a true but different portrait or perspective of the city. Chicago is a city with an exciting personality. And each approach to it brings out one aspect of that exciting personality.

Four Gospel Portraits

The four gospels are like the four approaches to the city of Chicago. They, too, are four different approaches to the same reality: the exciting, inspiring personality of Jesus. Just as each approach to the city of Chicago brings out a different aspect of the exciting personality of that city, so each gospel preserves a different aspect of the exciting personality of Jesus.

Let's take a close look at each of the four gospels. Let's try to see what aspect of the personality of Jesus each brings into sharper focus. Some years ago, I was studying in France. I had the opportunity to visit the famous Cathedral of Chartres, outside Paris. This 13th-century masterpiece contains over 1,800 stone statues of biblical figures. It is sometimes called a "Poor Man's Bible" in stone. On a Sunday afternoon, you can walk around it and relive every major event of the scriptures. Above the center door at Chartres is a remarkable stone sculpture. It was inspired by the fourth chapter of the Book of Revelation where John wrote:

I had another vision and saw an open door in heaven. . . . There in heaven was a throne with someone sitting on it. His face gleamed like such precious stones as jasper and carnelian. . . . Surrounding the throne . . . were four living creatures. . . . The first one looked like a lion; the second one like a bull; the third had a face like a man's face; the fourth looked like an eagle. . . . Day and night they never stopped singing: "Holy, holy, holy, is the Lord God Almighty, who was, who is, and who is to come."
(Revelations 4:1–3, 6–8)

Some ancient artists compared these four creatures to the four writers of the gospel: Matthew, Mark, Luke, and John. The desert lion was used to symbolize Mark because his gospel opens with a voice or cry in the desert. The sacrificial bull symbolized Luke because his gospel opens with sacrifice in the temple. The man symbolized Matthew because his gospel opens with a record of the human ancestry of Jesus. And, finally, the eagle symbolized John because his gospel opens with a soaring hymn of praise to Jesus, who, alone, looks on the face of God—just as the eagle soars high into the sky and, alone, looks on the face of the sun.

Now let's take a closer look at each gospel writer. Mark's gospel is symbolized by the desert lion because Mark opens his gospel with a voice or cry in the desert.

Mark's Portrait

Tradition says that Mark wrote his gospel in Rome about A.D. 65. This was at the time Christians were suffering persecution under Emperor Nero. Mark makes several references to persecution in his gospel. The big question in the minds of the persecuted Christians was why they were being asked to suffer and die for their new faith. Mark reminds them of two things. First, Jesus himself suffered. His suffering climaxed on Calvary. Mark tells us that a Roman soldier who saw how Jesus suffered and died was moved to faith. The soldier cried out: "This man was really the Son of God." Just as the suffering and death of Jesus brought faith to the Roman soldier, so the suffering and death of the early Christians eventually brought faith to the entire Roman Empire.

Second, Mark reminds his readers that Jesus taught his followers that they, too, must suffer: "If anyone wants to come with me," Jesus said, "he must forget himself, carry his cross, and follow me." In other words, Jesus says that anyone who wishes to follow him must be ready to suffer and die as he did.

Let me illustrate what Jesus was talking about with a story. There were two brothers in Georgia in the 1960s. Let's call the one John. He was a social worker and was deeply involved in interracial work. At the time, racial tensions in Georgia were high. Sit-ins were being held in restaurants. Marches were taking place. Black protestors and white sympathizers were being jailed. Soon John's interracial work came under fire. John and his friends needed legal help. They turned to John's brother. Let's call him Andrew. Andrew was a prominent lawyer and a Georgia politician. Andrew refused to get involved, saying that involvement could hurt his political future. John was shocked by Andrew's response. What shocked him most was that he and Andrew had once committed their lives together to Jesus. Andrew's response was hardly that of a committed Christian. John confronted Andrew about this. Andrew replied that he accepted Jesus. "I'm committed to Jesus," he said, "but I don't think this means I must also let myself be crucified as he was."

John looked at Andrew and said, "Andrew, you're not a follower of Jesus. You're only an admirer of his." As you might expect, John's remark caused his brother to do some deep soul-searching. "If anyone wants to come with me," said Jesus, "he must forget himself, carry his cross, and follow me." (Luke 8:34)

Suffering Savior

If we wish to follow Jesus, we must be prepared to carry our cross as he did. Mark's portrait of Jesus is that of the suffering savior.

Jesus does not suffer, and tell us to suffer, because suffering is something that is good. Absolutely not. Jesus suffered because helping people often involves suffering. If we are not willing to suffer, we will not be able to help others.

Think of a mother who realizes she will have to give up an enjoyable part-time job to devote more time to her handicapped child. Think of a father who realizes he will have to work two jobs to earn enough money to send his children to college. Think of a high school football star who realizes he will have to give up football for a part-time job because his father is sick and can't support the family. Mark's portrait of the suffering savior invites us to ask ourselves this question: "How ready are we to suffer for the sake of others, as Jesus did?"

There's another side to Jesus that Mark's portrait brings out. It is the forgiveness and compassion of Jesus for those who fall while trying to follow him. Nowhere is this illustrated more vividly than during his passion. After the soldiers arrested Jesus in the garden of Gethsemane, they took him to the house of the high priest. Peter followed at a distance. Later on, someone spotted Peter and identified him as one of the disciples of Jesus. Peter swore an oath, denying that he ever knew Jesus.

Why did Mark choose to record this unfortunate event? What good could it possibly serve? Mark probably included Peter's denial for a special reason. Mark wanted to remind Christians suffering persecution that if, like Peter, they denied Jesus under pressure, they could be forgiven, too, just as Peter was later forgiven by Jesus. So Mark's portrait of Jesus is an attractive one. Because Jesus suffered, he knows how suffering feels. And because Jesus knows how easy it is to fall under pressure, he has special compassion on us when we slip and fall in times of temptation.

Matthew's Portrait

That brings us to Matthew's gospel. Matthew's gospel is symbolized by a man because it opens with the human genealogy of Jesus.

Matthew's readers were primarily Jewish. One of their big questions was how does the life and the teaching of Jesus square with the teaching of the Hebrew Bible? In other words, how does the life and teaching of Jesus agree with what Moses and the prophets taught?

Matthew answered this important question in a variety of ways. For example, he went out of his way to show how the life of Jesus conformed with what the prophets foretold about the Messiah. Likewise, Matthew went out of his way to present the teaching of Jesus in five sections, just as the Jewish Torah presents the teaching of Moses. Jesus explained the close relationship between his own teaching and the Jewish scriptures this way:

"Do not think that I have come to do away with the Law of Moses and the teachings of the prophets. I have not come to do away with them, but to make their teachings come true."

(Matthew 5:17)

Teaching Savior

The portrait of Jesus that Matthew paints is that of the teaching savior. Jesus is the one foretold by the prophets. He is the one who brings the teachings of Moses to completion. The teachings of Jesus are not always easy to follow. Take this teaching:

"You have heard that it was said, 'Love your friends, hate your enemies.' But now I tell you: Love your enemies and pray for those who persecute you."

(Matthew 5:43-44)

A moving example of this teaching was reported in *Newsweek* magazine some years ago. What made me stop to read the article was the striking picture that accompanied it. It showed three brothers, ages 7 to 11, praying in a church. Jerry, the oldest brother, liked to listen to the news while he dressed for school. On one particular morning the news was very bad. Someone had planted a bomb on a commercial airliner. The bomb went off, causing the plane to crash, killing 44 persons. Jerry finished dressing, turned off the radio, and left his room for breakfast. As he started down the stairs, he saw his grandmother and the parish priest standing at the foot of the steps. He stopped, looked at both of them, and said: "Mom and Dad were on that plane, weren't they?" Jerry was right.

Later that day, students of St. Gabriel's school, which is the school Jerry and his brothers attended, asked their pastor for a prayer service for the parents of their three classmates. The pastor asked Jerry if this would be all right. Jerry said it would be. Then he added: "Could we pray, also, for the man who killed my mother and father?"

When someone hurts us deeply, our natural reaction is to respond with anger. Jerry's response illustrates the totally different response Jesus asked his followers to make. Jerry is inspiring proof that such a response can be made, if we open our hearts to the teaching savior of Matthew.

Luke's Portrait

Luke's gospel is symbolized by the sacrificial bull. That's because it opens with sacrifice in the temple. Luke wrote about the same time as Matthew. He wrote for Gentiles, that is, for non-Jews.

Many of these people were poor and rejected by their fellow citizens. Their big question was: What does Jesus say about us? Luke answered this question by telling them that Jesus himself was poor. He pointed out, also, that Jesus showed special concern for the poor. For example, on one occasion Jesus said:

> "Happy are you poor; the Kingdom of God is yours! Happy are you who are hungry now; you will be filled! Happy are you who weep now . . . a great reward is kept for you in heaven."
>
> (Luke 6:20-21, 23)

In other words, happy are you, for you have turned your plight into a stepping-stone to salvation by placing all your trust in my Father. Jesus does not present poverty as something good. Absolutely not! Rather, Jesus is saying, in effect, to the poor people of his time: "Don't let your misfortune crush you. Rather, crush your misfortune by using it to draw closer to God."

Compassionate Savior

The portrait of Jesus that Luke preserves for us is that of the compassionate savior. Not long ago, I was reminded of Luke's compassionate savior by an article in *Maryknoll* magazine. It was written by the mother of a South Korean poet whose name was Kim Chi Ha. She told how her son had just been sentenced to life in prison in South Korea. What crime did he commit? It was this. In a number of his recent poems he protested the government's treatment of the poor and oppressed! Kim Chi Ha's mother backed her son's position totally. She said: "Kim Chi Ha has said on many occasions . . . Jesus was always for the poor. . . . We, too, if we are followers of his, must be for the poor and the oppressed. . . . Society puts these people down, but the gospel tells us they are important. . . . We must take this world we live in seriously."

Kim Chi Ha never lost his deep-down joy and sense of humor throughout his ordeal. For example, when an angry judge added another seven years to his life sentence, Kim Chi Ha joked to his mother, "I must stay in prison seven years after I die!" Kim Chi Ha's mother ended her article, saying that she was proud of her son. She said that she was going to continue his work of speaking out in behalf of the poor and the oppressed.

John's Portrait

This brings us to the fourth gospel, John's gospel. This gospel is symbolized by the eagle because it begins with this soaring hymn of praise to Jesus:

Before the world was created, the Word already existed; he was with God, and he was the same as God. From the very beginning the Word was with God. Through him God made all things; not one thing in all creation was made without him. The Word was the source of life, and this life brought light to mankind. The light shines in the darkness, and the darkness has never put it out.

(John 1:1–5)

Early Christians called John "the theologian." They called his gospel "the spiritual gospel." From its first line to its last line it is strikingly different from the other gospels. For example, John does not use the story format often. When he does tell a story, he is more interested in the symbolism behind the story than in the story itself. For instance, after Jesus heals the man born blind, Jesus says: "I came to this world to judge, so that the blind could see and those who see should become blind." The blind man and the close-minded observers symbolize the two ways people still respond to the words and works of Jesus: if we are open to truth, we can begin to see, really see. If we are closed to truth, we might as well be blind.

Life-Giving Savior

The miracles of Jesus are signs of the new life that he gives to those who believe in him. Jesus is the "bread" of life. "Who eats this bread," Jesus says, "will live forever." Jesus is the "word" of life. "Who heeds this word," Jesus says, "will never die." Jesus is the "vine" of life. "Who remains united to me," Jesus says, "will bear much fruit." John's portrait of Jesus is that of the life-giving savior.

It can be summed up in these words of Jesus: "I have come in order that you may have life—life in all its fullness."

A modern illustration of the fullness of life Jesus promises to us, not just in the next life, but also in this life, is described beautifully in Keith Miller's book *A Taste of New Wine*. Keith's life had slowly turned stale on him. His job with a big oil company no longer challenged or excited him. Something was wrong, terribly wrong. One day Keith found himself in such a frightening state of desperation that he got into his company car and drove off into the countryside. After driving for a while, he pulled up on the side of the road, stopped the car, turned off the motor, and just sat there, staring off into space.

Keith had the philosophy that there was always one more bounce in the ball. After a couple of martinis and a good night's sleep, he could always start over the next morning. But now, there was no tomorrow morning for Keith. He had reached the end of his rope. He looked up at the sky and shouted to God, "If there is anything you want in this soul of mine, take it. I really mean it." That was years ago. But something came into Keith's life that day that never left him. There were no flashes of lightning, no claps of thunder, no mysterious voices. There was only the profound realization of what it is that God wants from us. Keith began to realize that God doesn't want our money. He doesn't want our life, even our whole life. He wants our will. And if we give him our will, he'll begin to show us life as we've never seen it before. It really is like being born again.

The Life-Giving Jesus

For the first time in his life, Keith Miller understood John's gospel portrait of Jesus, the "life-giving savior." It is this Jesus who promises love, joy, and hope, not only in the next life but also in this one. It is this Jesus who drives the darkness out of our lives and shows us the beauty that is really there. If you feel an emptiness or incompleteness in your life, if you don't experience the joy and the hope that should be in your heart, perhaps it is because you haven't yet opened your heart to the life-giving Jesus. It is this portrait of Jesus that John paints so beautifully in his gospel.

In this session together, we have looked at the four portraits of Jesus that the four evangelists preserve for us. First we saw the suffering savior of Mark, symbolized by the lion. Mark's portrait of Jesus highlights the fact that Jesus suffered to help others. It reminds us that if we wish to follow him, we must be ready to suffer to help others also. Recall the story of the two brothers in Georgia. Recall, also, the mother and her handicapped child, and the high school football captain who resigned from the team to help his family meet expenses.

Second, we saw the teaching savior of Matthew, symbolized by the man. Matthew's portrait of Jesus highlights the fact that Jesus brought to completion the teachings of Moses and the prophets. It reminds us that if we wish to follow Jesus, we must live out his teaching, no matter how hard it might be in certain circumstances. Recall Jerry and his request to pray for the man responsible for the death of his father and mother.

Third, we saw the compassionate savior of Luke, symbolized by the bull. Luke's portrait of Jesus highlights the fact that Jesus showed special concern for the poor and the outcasts. It reminds us that we, too, should reach out to those who have special need of our help. Recall the South Korean poet Kim Chi Ha and his mother.

Finally, we saw the life-giving savior of John, symbolized by the eagle. John's portrait of Jesus highlights the fact that Jesus came to make our lives fuller. It reminds us that if our lives seem empty, perhaps it is because we have not opened our hearts as we should to the life-giving savior of

John. Recall Keith Miller and the life that opened to him after he turned his life over to Jesus.

How to Study Jesus

The picture of Jesus that we have in the gospels is not a photograph, but a portrait. And we have not one portrait, but four, just as we have four different portraits of the city of Chicago. The best way to study Jesus, therefore, is to study the common features that cut across all four gospel portraits. In other words, what is there about the person and ministry of Jesus that each of the four evangelists, no matter the community or concern he was addressing, felt compelled to include in his gospel?

No visitor to Chicago would be content to view the city from a distance. Rather he would go into the city on foot. He would walk down Michigan Avenue. He would talk to its people. He would drink in all the experiences the city of Chicago has to offer.

We will try to do the same with Jesus in the chapters ahead. We will try to experience him completely. We will try to meet him in his total personality. We will explore the common features that cut across all four gospel portraits of Jesus: the suffering savior of Mark, the teaching savior of Matthew, the compassionate savior of Luke, and the life-giving savior of John.

Invitation to Seek Jesus

In other words, we will focus on the message and person of Jesus that the Holy Spirit inspired each evangelist to include in his gospel regardless of the audience for whom he wrote. It is this Jesus who wants to enter our lives—your life and my life—and enrich them in ways that we never dreamed possible.

To seek Jesus is the greatest of all human adventures. To find Jesus is the greatest of all human achievements. Won't you join us in the chapters ahead as we embark upon the greatest of all human endeavors: to seek and, with the grace of God, to find Jesus.

MEDITATION/DISCUSSION POINTS

1. The book says, "Just as the suffering and death of Jesus brought faith to the Roman soldier, so the suffering and death of the early Christians brought faith to the entire Roman Empire." Why does suffering move some people to faith when preaching won't? Recall a time when you suffered greatly. What gave you strength at that time?

2. The book says, "Mark probably included Peter's denial for a special reason." Recall the reason. Reflect on the example to illustrate how it still applies to us today.

3. Jesus says, "Happy are you poor; the Kingdom of God is yours!" Is Jesus teaching us that poverty is something desirable or good? If not, what is Jesus' point?

4. Jesus says, "Love your enemies and pray for those who persecute you." Recall a time when you prayed for someone who had harmed you, as the man who killed Jerry's father and mother harmed him.

5. Recall a time when, like Keith Miller, you were terribly depressed and ready to give up. What kept you going during the ordeal?

When Elizabeth heard Mary's greeting, the baby moved within her. Elizabeth was filled with the Holy Spirit and said in a loud voice, "You are the most blessed of all women, and blessed is the child you will bear!" *Luke 1:41-42*

4. EXPECTANCY OF JESUS

I don't usually read the letters to the editor of a magazine. But each December I do look at the letters to the editor of *Time* magazine. I'm always curious to see who its readers are nominating for the "Man or Woman of the Year."

The award is supposed to go to the person who has had the greatest impact on the year's news events. Reader suggestions range all over the ballpark. Some nominations are serious, and some are meant to be funny. Take 1982, for example. There were serious nominations, like the Sioux Falls woman who nominated the "peace activists" for warning us against nuclear armament. There were also humorous nominations, like the Savannah, Georgia, reader who nominated Pac Man and E.T.

But the winner was a real surprise. And here it is on the cover of *Time*. For the first time in the magazine's history the award was given not to a person but to the computer.

Man of the Year—44 B.C.

Time and times have really changed. If *Time* had been around in the decades prior to the birth of Jesus, one candidate for the "Man of the Year" in 44 B.C. would have been a shoo-in. That man was Julius Caesar. One ancient writer who knew Caesar described him as a man who was "most dynamic" in personality and character. He was open, frank, and extremely popular with his troops.

Another ancient writer says of Caesar: "He was skillful with sword and horse, and had amazing powers of physical endurance. He always was at the head of his army, walking more often than riding." Caesar's leadership ability took him to the top of the ladder in ancient Rome. He became the most popular man of his day.

But then came that fateful day in March in the year 44 B.C. It was three days before Caesar was to take a trip to the East. He had an appointment with the Roman Senate in Pompey's theater. The Senate's regular meeting hall was being repaired when Caesar arrived. He was greeted politely. Then something happened. A group of his political enemies rushed him. Seconds later, twenty-three daggers were plunged into his body.

A dying Caesar slumped helplessly into a pool of blood at the foot of Pompey's statue. In Caesar's hand, according to one report, was a note warning him of the assassination plot. Someone had handed it to him on his way to the theater, but Caesar didn't bother to read it. He was too involved in a conversation with Mark Antony at the time.

A Man Named Herod

Caesar's death touched off a power struggle for leadership of Rome. It eventually passed to Caesar's eighteen-year-old adopted son, Octavian. Octavian's victory was very bad news for at least one ancient ruler. That was a man named Herod the Great, the king of a small Roman province in far-off Judea.

Herod had actively supported one of Octavian's rivals. But Herod was a shrewd politician. He decided upon a bold move. As the story goes, Herod arranged an audience with Octavian. At the appropriate moment, Herod took off his crown and laid it at the feet of Octavian. This was his way of dramatizing that he was unworthy to serve an emperor whom he had opposed. Herod's gesture worked perfectly. Octavian picked up the crown and handed it back to Herod. He looked him straight in the eye and said, "Serve me as faithfully as you did my rival." Herod the Great did just that for the rest of his life.

Something Strange Happened

In 27 B.C. Octavian became Rome's first emperor. He took the name Augustus. This is the same Augustus mentioned by Luke. It is the same Augustus who ordered the Roman census at the time of the birth of Jesus. Something strange began to happen during the reign of Augustus. Historical records describe a widespread feeling of expectation among the common people. One scholar describes it this way: "There was something of a religious faith about it. . . . It was often associated with the figure of a 'Savior' or deliverer—a great man, perhaps a superman with something of divinity about him."

Millions of Romans thought this person might be Augustus himself. He brought unity and peace to a fragmented Roman world. But Augustus eventually faded into history, and so did Rome's expectation of a great leader.

Feeling of Expectation

The focus of history then shifted to the tiny province of Judea, where Herod the Great was still on the throne. In Judea, a similar feeling of expectation was stirring among the common people. Unlike the Roman masses, the Jewish masses could pinpoint a concrete reason for their expectation. Jews believed that the infinite God of all creation had revealed himself to Moses and to their prophets. This same God had rescued them from slavery in Egypt and, again, from slavery in Babylonia. Jewish holy men and Jewish holy books kept alive these rich memories of Israel's past.

And now a new wind began to blow. An exciting hope began to build. People began to sense, deep down in their bones, that God was going to act again, in their behalf, soon. This new hope found expression in the Book of Daniel. There Daniel spoke of the coming of a great day and a great king. In the popular mind this king would catapult Israel into first place among the nations of the world. He would be an "Anointed Person," like the great King David. He would be a kind of Julius Caesar for the Jewish nation. The Jews gave to this hoped-for king the title Messiah.

God's Power Will Rest upon You

Now, let's keep in mind this mood of expectation as we listen to a reading of the opening chapter of Luke's Gospel:

During the time when Herod was king of Judea . . . God sent the angel Gabriel to a town in Galilee named Nazareth. He had a message for a girl promised in marriage to a man named Joseph, who was a descendant of King David. The girl's name was Mary. The angel came to her and said, "Peace be with you! The Lord is with you and has greatly blessed you!"

Mary was deeply troubled by the angel's message, and she wondered what his words meant. The angel said to her, "Don't be afraid, Mary; God has been gracious to you. You will become pregnant and give birth to a son, and you will name him

Jesus. He will be great and will be called the Son of the Most High God. The Lord God will make him a king, as his ancestor David was, and he will be the king of the descendants of Jacob forever; his kingdom will never end!"

Mary said to the angel, "I am a virgin. How, then, can this be?"

The angel answered, "The Holy Spirit will come on you, and God's power will rest upon you. For this reason the holy child will be called the Son of God. Remember your relative Elizabeth. It is said that she cannot have children, but she herself is now six months pregnant, even though she is very old. For there is nothing that God cannot do."

"I am the Lord's servant," said Mary; "may it happen to me as you have said."

(Luke 1:5, 26–38)

Years ago, when I began my studies for the ministry, one of my first spiritual experiences was a month-long silent retreat. For thirty days, I lived in seclusion and spent five hours daily, in five separate sessions, meditating on the life of Jesus.

Every day my spiritual director gave me a passage from the gospel to meditate on. He also gave me some advice on how to proceed with my meditation. I'll never forget one of his suggestions. It concerned the gospel passage just read. His advice went something like this: "Imagine yourself 2,000 years back in time. You are looking down from space on planet Earth. Suddenly you recognize the Holy Land and town of Nazareth. You also see Mary praying there. As you look on, an angel appears to Mary. The angel tells Mary that she will bear a child, who is to be called Jesus."

My spiritual director told me to pay special attention to the words that were spoken on that occasion. In hindsight, I see why he told me this. Take, for example, these words of the angel to Mary: "The Holy Spirit will come on you, and God's power will rest upon you. For this reason the holy child will be called the Son of God."

God's Covenant Presence

The expression "rest upon," also translated as "cover" or "overshadow," is found only rarely in the Bible. But one place you find it is in the Book of Exodus. There it describes the mysterious cloud that "rested upon" or "covered" the meeting tent of Israel. The meeting tent is where the Hebrews kept the container that housed the stone tablets on which were written the Ten Commandments. The movie *Raiders of the Lost Ark* dealt with the search for this lost container. It is also referred to as the "Ark of the Covenant" or the "Covenant Box."

Now let's see how the Book of Exodus describes all of this.

The LORD said to Moses, ". . . Set up the tent. . . . Place in it the Covenant Box containing the Ten Commandments. . . ." Moses did everything just as the Lord commanded. . . . Then a cloud covered the Tent and the dazzling light of the LORD's presence filled it."

(Exodus 40:1–3, 16, 34)

God's Presence in Mary

Now, here's the key point. Just as the cloud is portrayed as overshadowing the tent and filling it with the divine presence, so the Holy Spirit is portrayed as overshadowing Mary and filling her with the divine presence. And what was the divine presence in Mary? It was the child Jesus. Jesus himself is the divine presence. The point of Luke's passage seems to be this. The glory of God now resides in Israel, not just in the symbol of the ark, but in the person of Jesus, housed in the womb of the virgin Mary.

Let's digress for a moment so that I can develop the idea of presence. God can be present to us in different ways, just as people can be present to each other in different ways. For example, a son away at college can be present to his mother by a photograph, by a letter, or by his belongings in his bedroom. When her son comes home, he becomes present to her in person, that is, bodily.

God's Presence in Creation

In a similar way, God is present to us in the cosmos, which he created. God brought every-thing into existence—the stars, the mountains, and the seas. The Book of Genesis describes the beginning of God's presence in the cosmos this way:

Everything was engulfed in total darkness, and the power of God was moving over the water. Then God commanded, "Let there be light!"
(Genesis 1:2-3)

So the power of God is described as moving over the water, just as the cloud moved over the tent and the Holy Spirit moved over Mary.

It is interesting that the Bible describes God's becoming present among us in his covenant and in Jesus. In each case, a new presence of God among his people begins. In the case of creation, God is present in our cosmos not merely because he created it but also because he continues to hold it in existence day after day.

I like to compare God's presence in our cosmos to a movie projector that casts an image on a screen. The image owes its existence to the projector. Furthermore, the image stays alive on the screen only as long as the movie projector keeps it there.

It is the same with the created cosmos. God gave it existence and continues to hold it in existence. If God stopped holding it in existence, it would cease to be.

God's Presence among Us

And so God's first presence among us might be called his cosmic presence, that is, his presence among us by his creation. Second, God is present to us through his covenant. This is the covenant we read about in the Bible. It is God's revelation of himself by his word first to Israel and then, through Israel, to all nations. And third, God is present to us through his Son, Jesus. Jesus entered our world at the very moment the Holy Spirit overshadowed Mary.

This is such an important point; let me repeat it. The three main ways God is present among us are: his cosmic presence, that is, by the created cosmos; his covenant presence, that is, by the revelation of his word to Israel; and his incarnate presence, that is, his only Son, Jesus.

God's cosmic presence began when the power of God overshadowed the darkness and God said, "Let there be light!" God's covenant presence began when the cloud overshadowed the meeting tent and God filled it with his glory. God's incarnate presence—that is, presence in human form—began when the Holy Spirit overshadowed Mary and said, "You will give birth to a son."

Let's now return to the annunciation narrative. Soon after Mary conceived Jesus by the power of the Holy Spirit, she went to the house of Zechariah to visit her cousin Elizabeth. Elizabeth was also with child. She would soon give birth to John the Baptist.

[Mary] went into Zechariah's house and greeted Elizabeth. When Elizabeth heard Mary's greeting, the baby moved within her. Elizabeth was filled with the Holy Spirit and said in a loud voice, "You are most blessed of all women, and blessed is the child you will bear! Why should this great thing happen to me, that my Lord's mother comes to visit me? For as soon as I heard your greeting, the baby within me jumped with gladness. How happy you are to believe that the Lord's message to you will come true!"

(Luke 1:40–45)

Impact of Jesus

There is nothing unusual about a baby moving about in a mother's womb. But in this case, Luke intends the infant's movement to be a dramatic response to the presence of Jesus in Mary's womb. The movement of John within Elizabeth's womb gives us a kind of preview of the powerful impact that the presence of Jesus will have on people in his future ministry. Let me illustrate with just two examples.

The first took place early in the ministry of Jesus on the Sea of Galilee. Peter and Andrew had just returned from fishing. They had been out all night and had caught nothing. Jesus then told them to lower their nets a final time:

"Master," Simon answered, "we worked hard all night and caught nothing. But if you say so, I will let down the nets." They let them down and caught such a large number of fish that the nets were about to break. So they motioned to their partners in the other boat to come and help them. They came and filled both boats so full of fish that the boats were about to sink. When Simon Peter saw what had happened, he fell on his knees before Jesus and said, "Go away from me, Lord! I am a sinful man!"

(Luke 5:5-8)

In other words, at that moment, Peter sensed that overwhelming holiness of God in Jesus in a way that he had never experienced before.

The second example took place one day when Jesus went up a mountain to pray. He took with him Peter, James, and John.

[Suddenly] a change came over Jesus: his face was shining like the sun, and his clothes were dazzling white. Then the three disciples saw Moses and Elijah talking with Jesus. So Peter spoke up and said to Jesus, "Lord, how good it is that we are here! . . ." While he was talking, a shining cloud came over them, and a voice from the cloud said, "This is my own dear Son, with whom I am pleased—listen to him!" When the disciples heard the voice, they were so terrified that they threw themselves face downward on the ground.

(Matthew 17:2-6)

For a brief moment, Peter, James, and John experienced a part of Jesus that they had never experienced before. It was a moment they would never forget. Years later Peter wrote:

With our own eyes we saw his greatness. We were there ... when the voice came to him.... We ourselves heard this voice ... when we were with him on the holy mountain.

(2 Peter 1:16–18)

What Peter experienced in Jesus on the seashore, and what Peter, James, and John experienced on the mountain, continued to be experienced by people even after Jesus' lifetime. Recall Paul's experience of Jesus on the road to Damascus:

A light from the sky flashed around him. He fell to the ground and heard a voice saying to him, "Saul, Saul! Why do you persecute me?" "Who are you, Lord?" Paul asked. "I am Jesus, whom you persecute," the voice said.

(Acts 9:3–5)

Modern Impact of Jesus

Two thousand years later, the presence of Jesus still has a powerful impact on people. Take the case of Starr Daily. He was one of the early pioneers of prison reform in our country. Starr Daily was once a hard-core criminal. He was a hopeless case. When a judge sentenced him to prison for a third time, the judge said, "More punishment is not the remedy. I don't know what else to do. Our helplessness is your hopelessness."

This time Daily's prison behavior became so bad that he was thrown into "the hole," the worst kind of solitary confinement. Usually a prisoner lasts only two weeks in the hole. But this period came and went for Daily. Later Daily said of the ordeal, "I seemed to be sustained by hate alone."

As Daily lay on the icy floor of the hole, something strange began to stir within him. He suddenly wondered what would have happened had he dedicated his life to good rather than to evil. What happened next, he said, is hard to describe. But as best he could recall, he experienced the powerful presence of Jesus in a remarkable way. "In all my life," he wrote later, "I had never felt such love as I did during that experience. . . . Before that experience I was a calloused criminal; after it I was completely healed of my criminal tendencies."

Like Peter on the seashore, like Peter, James, and John on the mountain, and like Paul on the road to Damascus, Daily experienced the presence of Jesus in a powerful way. It was an experience that changed his life in the most remarkable way imaginable.

Community Impact of Jesus

I have one final favorite story of the powerful impact that the risen Jesus still has on people who open their hearts to him. This is the story of the prisoners of war in the Kwai Noi River camp in Thailand during World War II. I like it, especially, because it is a story of a large group of prisoners, not just one isolated person, who experienced the presence of Jesus in their midst in a remarkable way.

The situation of prisoners in the Kwai Noi camp had become desperate. It was not just the prison officials but prisoners themselves who had turned the camp into a living hell. One eyewitness wrote, "The jungle law of survival . . . took over. Men stole one another's food. . . . Some resorted to treachery. . . . [Our Asian captors] found it amusing to watch the once-proud white soldiers destroying one another."

Then a remarkable change took place. It began with a few prisoners coming together to read and meditate on the gospels. One prisoner said of the change, "[It was] one of the most wondrous changes I ever witnessed. Not me alone, but the entire camp of 3,000 men. . . . The focal point of all this activity was the church [that we had built out of] bamboo and jungle grass. . . . [We placed in it] a rough wooden cross on a bamboo altar, its very shape drawing suffering men's gaze upward toward God and outward toward mankind. 'Wherever two or three are gathered in my name,' said Jesus, 'I am there with them.' "

The experience of these men is just one more example of the powerful impact Jesus still has on people right up into modern times. I am sure some of you have experienced the powerful impact of Jesus in your own lives.

Interrelated Roles

Let's now return to the expectancy of Jesus as Luke describes it for us in the first chapter of his gospel. After Elizabeth told Mary how the child in her womb had leaped at the presence of Jesus, Mary sang out, "My heart praises the Lord; my soul is glad because of God my Savior for he has remembered me, his lowly servant."

Here we have another example of something that occurs over and over in scripture. The people God picks to do his work are often those who are considered unimportant by the world. God seems to have a special love for the ordinary people of the world.

Luke concludes his annunciation narrative by describing the birth of John the Baptist. This leads us to an interesting point about the writing style Luke used in the early chapters of his gospel. He employs a technique that is used frequently in modern TV drama. This technique is to present several stories at the same time, switching back and forth, relating them to one another.

In other words, Luke switches back and forth between the stories of John and Jesus. For example, the birth announcement of John is followed by the birth announcement of Jesus; the birth of John is followed by the birth of Jesus; the youth of John is followed by the youth of Jesus; and, finally, the ministry of John is followed by the ministry of Jesus.

Luke's reason for interweaving these stories is to point out the interrelated roles Jesus and John play in the salvation of the world. John prepares the world for Jesus. Jesus saves the world from sin.

The Stage Is Set

And so, step by step, the stage of history was prepared for the birth of Jesus. We saw how this preparation began with a mood of expectation among the masses in Rome and in Judea. Next, we saw how the mood of expectation died in Rome when Augustus died. Finally, we saw how the mood of expectation grew in Judea.

It was against this backdrop of expectation that we read the opening chapter of the Gospel according to Luke. In that chapter Luke made two points. First, Luke described the descent of the Holy Spirit upon Mary. His point was to reveal that a new presence of God was about to begin on earth. God was about to take up residence among his people in the person of Jesus.

Second, Luke described Mary's visit to Elizabeth, and how Jesus caused John to leap in the womb of Elizabeth. Luke's point was to preview for us the powerful impact that the presence of Jesus would have on people, not only in his own day but also in ours.

We saw the power of this impact on Peter at the seashore; on Peter, James, and John on the mountain; on Paul on the road to Damascus; on Starr Daily in prison; and on the 3,000 soldiers in the Kwai Noi River camp in Thailand.

Man of the Year—1 B.C.

From the hindsight of history, if we make Julius Caesar the "Man of the Year" for 44 B.C., we should make John the Baptist the "Man of the Year" for 1 B.C. For John is the first person, apart from Mary, to experience the power of Jesus in the world. And it is John, too, who prepared us to open our hearts to the presence of Jesus.

Let's now listen to the words that John's father, Zechariah, used to praise God after John's birth:

"You, my child, will be called a prophet of the Most High God. . . . He will cause the bright dawn of salvation to rise on us and to shine from heaven on all those who live in the dark shadow of death, to guide our steps into the path of peace."

(Luke 1:76, 78–79)

MEDITATION/DISCUSSION POINTS

1. The angel told Mary she would give birth to a child. Mary didn't see how this was possible.

She said, "I am a virgin. How, then, can this be?" Reflect on a time when your faith in God or God's word was tested.

2. The leaping of John in Elizabeth's womb acted as a "kind of preview of the powerful impact that the presence of Jesus would have on people in his future ministry." Reflect on a time when you experienced Jesus' presence in a special way in another person.

3. Recall a time when you experienced Jesus' presence in a special way in a group setting, as did the prisoners in the Kwai Noi camp.

4. Recall a time when you experienced Jesus' presence in a special way when you were all alone, as when Starr Daily was in "the hole."

5. The book says: " Octavian picked up the crown and handed it back to Herod [a friend of Octavian's political rival]. He looked him straight in the eye and said, 'Serve me as faithfully as you did my rival.'" Recall a time when you were forgiven by a rival or when a rival forgave you.

The Word became a human being and, full of grace and truth, lived among us. We saw his glory, the glory which he received as the Father's only Son. *John 1:14*

5. BIRTH OF JESUS

Some years ago, during a trip to the Holy Land, James Martin bought a nativity set in Bethlehem. All the figures were there: Jesus, Mary, Joseph, the shepherds. When Martin arrived at the Tel Aviv airport for his return trip to the United States, security was especially tight. The customs officers carefully checked and x-rayed each figure, even the baby Jesus.

"We can't take any chances," the officer told Martin. "We have to make sure that there is nothing explosive in this set!" Afterward, Martin thought to himself, "If the officer only knew! That set contains the most explosive force in our world!"

God Loves Us!

What is the explosive force or power contained in the scene portraying the birth of Jesus? You know what it is. I know what it is. It is the incredible revelation that God loves us so much that he became one of us and lived among us. It is really hard for us to imagine that the creator of this vast cosmos, out of love for us, you and me, at a point in time crossed an unimaginable border and was born as a little baby on this tiny planet we call earth.

In the face of this mystery, my intellect sputters and comes to a halt. But one day, a friend gave me a clue that helped my understanding more than anything else. She simply said, "Well, love does such things."

Unfortunately, we Christians are so used to hearing the statement "God loves us," that it hardly registers anymore. We hear it with our ears. We accept it with our minds. But it doesn't really touch our hearts. I remember when I was a student studying for the ministry, one of my teachers said to me, "Mark, the day you become aware in your heart that God loves you, personally, your life will take a leap forward as you never dreamed possible."

Turning Point

I envied my teacher's ability to say that. I knew exactly what he meant. I believed intellectually that God loved me. But the impact of his love had never fully made its way down from my head to my heart. The day that it did was a turning point in my life. It deepened in a profound way my appreciation of myself, other people, and life itself. Nothing had changed, and yet everything had changed! It was literally the feeling you get when you fall in love for the first time.

How God Shows His Love

But there's also a second source of power in the Christmas scene. It is the power contained in the way God chose to reveal his love for us. God didn't send a letter. He didn't send a prophet. He didn't send an angel. He sent his Son! And he sent his Son not as a powerful prince born in a palace in one of the supernations of the world. No! He sent him as a weak baby born in a manger in one of the small nations of the world.

It is hard for us to appreciate this incredible story of the way God chose to become one of us. We've heard it so often! But just for this one time, let's try to listen to the Christmas story as though we were hearing it for the very first time. Let's try to listen to it as children do. Let's try to listen to it the way the first Christians did. Let's try to listen to it the way people for 2,000 years have passed it on from one generation to the next.

At that time Emperor Augustus ordered a census to be taken throughout the Roman Empire. . . . Joseph went from the town of Nazareth in Galilee to the town of Bethlehem in Judea, the birthplace of King David. Joseph was there because he was a descendant of David. He went to register with Mary who was promised in marriage to him. She was pregnant, and while they were in Bethlehem, the time came for her to have her baby. She gave birth to her first son, wrapped him in cloths and laid him in a manger—there was no room for them to stay in the inn.

(Luke 2:1, 4–7)

As I listen to that incredibly simple story, I can't help but think that this was really the ideal way for Jesus to be born. How else could he have said "I love you" more perfectly than by being born in such humble circumstances? Even a child can understand the awesome message behind the humble and simple birth of Jesus. And because Jesus entered our world as the most ordinary of people, we can relate to him in a human and personal way. He is, indeed, one of us.

Jesus Speaks to the Heart

Seeing Jesus in this vulnerable situation speaks to us in a special way. It speaks to our heart. It makes Jesus more credible, more real. Like us, he entered the world in the same helpless, vulnerable way. Like us, he had to learn how to stand, how to walk, how to talk.

I'd like to digress here for a minute to tell you one of my favorite stories. At first, you may wonder how it relates to the birth of Jesus. But as it develops, you will see how relevant it really is. This is a true story about Ron Santo, the former home-run-hitting third baseman of the Chicago Cubs. If you are a baseball fan, as I am, you may remember him well.

On one of his days off, Santo was working with a group of diabetic children at Lake Geneva, Wisconsin. He caught them completely off guard by telling that he, too, was a diabetic. For thirteen years he had kept this secret from the public. Santo told the wide-eyed youngsters, "I give myself an injection [of insulin] at a specific time each day, depending on whether we are playing a day or night game. And I keep candy and instant sugar handy at the ball park in case of emergencies."

Suddenly the kids wanted to grab him and hug him. They no longer thought of him as a faraway hero, an all-star third baseman for the Chicago Cubs. To these kids he was a diabetic just like them. He could understand their feelings, and they could understand his feelings. The kids felt an identity with Ron Santo that only fellow diabetics could feel. They drew exciting new hope from his presence. If he could achieve great things in spite of his affliction, so could they. Ron Santo had suddenly changed their world from one whose horizon was filled with storm clouds to one that was filled with sunlight.

Jesus Brings Hope

This brings us back to the story of the birth of Jesus. Because God chose to become one of us, even to the point of sharing our physical weaknesses, we are able to identify with him just as the diabetic children were able to identify with Ron Santo.

We are able to do much more. We are able to draw exciting new hope from Jesus. If he could do what he did in spite of his human situation, so can we. Just as Santo changed the world of those diabetic children, so Jesus changed our world. Jesus brought new hope into a world where hope had almost died out completely for some people. This is the explosive power contained in the Christmas story.

God Chose the Weak

But the Christmas story's explosive power doesn't stop here; it goes even further. Besides the power contained in the revelation that God loves us, and besides the power contained in the way God revealed his love for us, there is the power contained in the people God picked to greet his Son after his birth. God didn't choose kings, or scholars, or religious leaders. Rather, he chose insignificant people, those who had no clout, no bank account, no friends in high places.

There were some shepherds in that part of the country who were spending the night in the fields, taking care of their flocks. An angel of the Lord appeared to them, and the glory of the Lord shone over them. They were terribly afraid, but the angel said to them, "Don't be afraid! I am here with good news for you, which will bring great joy to all the people. This very day in David's town your Savior was born—Christ the Lord! And this is what will prove it to you: you will find a baby wrapped in cloths and lying in a manger." . . . So they hurried

off and found Mary and Joseph and saw the baby
lying in the manger.

(Luke 2:8-12, 16)

It comes as a surprise to a lot of people that
these shepherds who came to visit Jesus were not
gentle country folk. For centuries we have made
them out to be lovable herders of sheep. The fact
is that they were despised outcasts. Here's how
one historian described them: "Shepherds had
the very worst reputation. They were tough char-
acters who fearlessly bashed in the heads of
wolves that came bothering their flocks and
would not have hesitated to do the same for
Scribes or Pharisees who came bothering their
consciences. These despised rustics were ex-
cluded from the law courts. . . . Their testimony
was not admitted in a trial."

Why the Weak?

It is deeply significant that God chose these outcasts to be the first people to greet his Son. But
here again, when you think about it, it really
makes sense that the first people to meet Jesus
should be outcasts and sinners. For these misfits
and sinners of society needed to know, more than
anyone, that even though they were rejected by
men, they were loved by God. How better could
God show his love for them than to invite them to
be the first people to meet his Son?

The presence of these outcasts at the birth of
Jesus tips us off to something that Luke stresses
over and over again in his gospel. It is that Jesus
goes out of his way to identify with the poor and
rejected of his day.

Not long ago, I ran across a story in *Maryknoll*
magazine about some poor, outcast people in our

modern world. A missionary, Paul Newpower, was describing how Indians in the mountains of Bolivia celebrate Christmas. The highlight of their celebration isn't decorating a tree. It isn't exchanging gifts. It isn't singing Christmas carols. The highlight of their celebration is the Sheep's Mass. That's right, the Sheep's Mass.

Missionary Paul Newpower's first experience of this unusual celebration really threw him. When he walked into church on Christmas morning, the huge old Spanish cathedral was already swarming with Indian children. He was horrified to discover that every child had brought along a lamb. They had decorated the lambs by tying tiny bits of colored wool around their ears, tails, and legs. The tiny lambs really looked like walking Christmas trees. But even though this was a touching sight, all the missionary could think about was the noise and the confusion created by the lambs and the children.

To make a long story short, Newpower braced himself and celebrated the Sheep's Mass. To his way of thinking, the Mass was a total disaster. The noise, the confusion, and the stench revolted him. People were milling around. Kids were playing with their lambs. It was awful. His carefully prepared Christmas message was completely drowned out by the constant *ba-a-a-a*'s of the lambs. Even the incense was overpowered by other odors.

By the time the missionary finished Christmas services, he was really upset. Afterward he complained to an Indian friend, "What does all this have to do with Christmas?" His Indian friend replied, "Don't you remember, Father? The first people to visit Jesus were shepherds. They didn't want to leave their newborn lambs unattended, so they brought them along. And together with the lambs, they greeted the newborn Jesus. We're shepherds, and this is how we celebrate the great day when God came to live among us."

Father Newpower was really stunned by his friend's response. Then, slowly, he began to see his friend's point of view. The missionary left the church that Christmas morning realizing that the *ba-a-a-a*'s of the lambs had preached a far better sermon than he had. Now he began to have some notion of what Christmas was all about.

And so the explosive power of the Christmas scene consists of three incredible revelations. First, God loves us. Second, God revealed his love for us by sending his Son, Jesus, to tell us about his love. Third, God chose sinners to be the first people to greet his Son.

Matthew's Birth Story

Let's now move from Luke's account of the birth of Jesus to Matthew's. As you know, Luke and Matthew are the only two evangelists who write about the birth of Jesus. Matthew begins his account of the Christmas story almost at the very place where Luke leaves off. He begins it, saying: "Jesus was born in the town of Bethlehem in Judea, during the time Herod was King of Judea." Then Matthew writes:

Soon afterward, some men who studied the stars came from the East to Jerusalem and asked, "Where is the baby born to be the king of the Jews? We saw his star when it came up in the east, and we have come to worship him."

(Matthew 2:1–2)

After making inquiries from his advisers, Herod directs them to Bethlehem. When the men from the East find Jesus, Matthew says, "They brought out their gifts of gold, frankincense, and myrrh, and presented them to him."

The gift-giving recalls the words of Psalm 72:

The kings of Spain and of the islands will offer him gifts. The kings of Arabia and Ethiopia will bring him offerings. All kings will bow down before him; all nations will serve him.

(Psalm 72:10-11)

No doubt this Psalm explains why artists often portray the visitors as kings. Actually Matthew says nothing about kings. He calls them "men who studied the stars."

Matthew's reference to three gifts—gold, frankincense, and myrrh—explains why artists usually place the number of visitors at three. Actually Matthew does not say how many visitors there were. True, most modern artists show three visitors, but ancient artists showed as many as nine and as few as two.

Humanity of Jesus

Christians interpret the gifts of gold, frankincense, and myrrh in a number of symbolic ways. For example, many think myrrh may symbolize the humanity of Jesus. One use of myrrh among ancients was to prepare the dead for burial. For example, the women brought myrrh to the tomb of Jesus. Because of myrrh's relationship to death, it makes a vivid symbol of our human vulnerability.

The gift of myrrh reminds us that Jesus was human, like you and I. It reminds us that Jesus experienced all the human emotions that we experience. For example, Jesus felt moments of great joy. After his disciples return enthusiastically from a mission of teaching and healing, Luke says, "Jesus was filled with joy by the Holy Spirit." (Luke 10:21)

Jesus also experienced moments of anguish and depression. In the garden of Gethsemane, he said to his disciples, "The sorrow in my heart is so great that it almost crushes me." (Mark 14:34)

Jesus also experienced moments of great loneliness when everyone, even God, seemed to desert him. On the cross, he cried out in the words of Psalm 22, "My God, my God, why have you abandoned me?" (Psalm 22:1) Yes, Jesus was human like us. As a result, he experienced the same human emotions that all of us experience.

Divinity of Jesus

The gift of frankincense symbolizes the divinity of Jesus. From ancient times people have used incense in religious worship. The aroma and the smoke ascending upward speak of divinity. Early Christians saw the gift of incense as a symbol of the divinity of Jesus. Jesus is both God and man. Paul writes in Philippians 2:

[Jesus] always had the nature of God, but he . . . became like man and appeared in human likeness. He was humble and walked the path of obedience all the way to death—his death on the cross. For this reason God raised him to the highest place above.

(Philippians 2:6–9)

Kingship of Jesus

Christians throughout the centuries have interpreted the gift of gold to be a symbol of the kingship of Jesus. To understand the role of Jesus as king, we need to understand the role that a king played in ancient society. A king was, above all, a leader of people. The ideal king was one who led his people by love. He was one who undertook noble causes for his people. The ideal king was also one who could inspire his people to join him in his work.

Jesus was such a king. He is someone who leads by love. He is someone who has undertaken the noblest of all causes, the establishment of God's Kingdom on earth. And Jesus is someone who inspires and invites us to join him.

What Is God's Kingdom?

In ordinary, everyday terms, what do we mean by the establishment of God's Kingdom on earth? We mean the creation of a whole new environment in the world—an environment in which love will replace hate, light will replace darkness, care will replace neglect, and life will replace death. We mean the creation of an environment in which the hungry man, the thirsty woman, the naked child—these will find caring brothers and sisters where before they found only strangers passing them without care, like a ship in the night.

It is for the establishment of God's Kingdom—this environment of love and care—that Jesus invites you and me to pray daily, "Thy Kingdom come, thy will be done on earth as it is in heaven." It is for the establishment of God's Kingdom—this environment of care and concern—

that Jesus invites you and me to carry out the final instructions that he gave us.

"Go, then, to all peoples everywhere and make them my disciples: baptize them in the name of the Father, the Son, and the Holy Spirit, and teach them to obey everything I have commanded you. And I will be with you always to the end of the age."

(Matthew 28:19-20)

It is true that God's Kingdom seems very idealistic and far removed from the real world. Actually it is neither. You and I know that as individuals we possess an enormous, untapped potential for good in our hearts. We know that we live our lives by making choices. The Kingdom of God is nothing more or less than each of us choosing to live our lives as God intended us to live them, and as Jesus gave us the power to live them.

The Kingdom of God is not something out there. It is something in here. "The Kingdom of God is within you," Jesus said. The Kingdom of God is in the human heart, your heart and my heart. If the Kingdom of God does not seem to be coming about in modern times, perhaps it is because we, the followers of Jesus, have not prayed and have not worked as we should. We have not yet really established the Kingdom of God in our own hearts.

What Can I Do?

If you're like me, you sometimes ask yourself, "What am I doing to advance God's Kingdom in my own home, in the place where I work, in the neighborhood where I live—right now, at this time in my life? What keeps me from doing more to advance God's Kingdom?"

Because God made us in his image, he does not impose his will on us. We are free to choose. The Kingdom of God will come about only when each of us and all of us choose to do something about it. We know what we must do. But we must do it ourselves. God will not do it for us. We must make a personal choice. We must choose Jesus and God's Kingdom freely.

The Christmas stories of Luke and Matthew do, indeed, contain an explosive power. Luke's story teaches us three incredible truths. First, God loves us. Second, God sent his Son, Jesus, to tell us about his love. Third, God chose sinners to be the first to greet his Son.

Because of the incredible way God chose to reveal his love for us, we can relate to his Son in a deeply personal way. We can do much more. We can draw exciting new hope from his Son. If Jesus could do what he did, in spite of his human situation, so can we.

Matthew's story picks up where Luke's story leaves off. It focuses mainly on the Gentile visitors from the East. It teaches us that Jesus is not only the long-awaited Messiah of the Jews but also the Savior of all peoples.

We saw also how the three gifts of these Gentile visitors can be interpreted to reveal three truths about Jesus. First, the myrrh symbolizes the humanity of Jesus. Jesus is totally and truly human, just as you and I are.

Second, the frankincense symbolizes the divinity of Jesus. Jesus is totally and truly God.

Third, the gold symbolizes the kingship of Jesus. Jesus came among us to lead us, to inspire us, to invite us to join him in bringing about

God's Kingdom on earth—a kingdom of love, and kingdom of peace, a kingdom of hope.

Earlier in the chapter, I asked you to try to listen to the Christmas story as though you were hearing it for the first time. I asked you to try to listen to it as the first Christians listened to it. I asked you to try to listen to it the way children listen to it.

Jesus' Invitation

Today, Christmas has become so obscured with parties and other celebrations that it has all but lost its true meaning. We need to be challenged anew by the Christmas story, just as the missionary was challenged anew by the way the Indians of Bolivia celebrated Christmas. We need to hear anew the "Good News" of Christmas in all its original power.

And what is that "Good News"? It is this: The great God of all creation, in the person of Jesus, has come to live among us and invite us, you and me, to join him in creating a new world. And what is this new world? It is a world in which there will be no more tears or grief or pain—one in which the needy man and the needy woman will find brothers and sisters where before they found only strangers.

"When the song of the angels is stilled, when the star in the sky is gone, when the kings and princes are home, when the shepherds are back with the flocks, the work of Christmas begins: to find the lost, to heal the broken, to feed the hungry, to release the prisoners, to rebuild the nations, to bring peace among brothers, to make music in the heart."

MEDITATION/DISCUSSION POINTS

1. The author says, "I believed intellectually that God loved me. But the impact of his love had never fully made its way down from my head to my heart." To what extent has your own appreciation of God's love made its way down from your head to your heart?

2. Reflect on ways your own present life would be different had Jesus not entered our world as one of us.

3. The book says, "Suddenly the kids wanted to grab him (Ron Santo) and hug him. They no longer thought of him as a faraway hero. . . . He was a diabetic just like them." To what extent do you relate to Jesus like this because he became one of us?

4. Missionary Paul Newpower "left the church that Christmas morning realizing that the *ba-a-a-a*'s of the lambs had preached a far better sermon than he had." Recall a sermon that made a deep impression on you.

5. The author says, "If you're like me you sometimes ask yourself, 'What am I doing to advance God's Kingdom . . . right now, at this time in my life?'" What are some of the things you are doing right how in your life?

After all the people had been baptized, Jesus also was baptized. While he was praying, heaven was opened, and the Holy Spirit came down upon him in bodily form like a dove. *Luke 3:21–22*

6. BAPTISM OF JESUS

Author Philip Yancey was on a plane. It had just taken off from Philadelphia. Yancey looked out the window for a while. Then he opened his briefcase and pulled out a copy of the book *Night*. It is a true story by Elie Wiesel. Elie was only fifteen years old when he was imprisoned in a Nazi concentration camp in World War II.

The people of Elie's hometown in Hungary had no idea what was going on in these camps. Their first indication that something horrible might be taking place came from a happy-go-lucky little Jew named Moche. Moche used to live in the town, but he had been arrested and taken away by the Nazis because he was not a native Hungarian.

Moche's Story

Then, one night, Moche surprised everyone by showing up again. But now, he was no longer happy-go-lucky. He was sad and depressed. Something had changed. "What happened to you, Moche?" somebody asked. A faraway look came to Moche's eyes, and then he began to tell his story. He was taken with other Jews to a prison camp in Poland. There, they were put to work digging a big pit. When the pit was finished, the prisoners were machine-gunned and buried in the very hole they had dug. Moche had miraculously survived.

When Moche finished his story, everyone looked at him in disbelief. They asked a few questions, shook their heads, and went on their way. After they left, Moche said to himself, "They didn't believe me."

Later, Moche repeated his story to others. Their reaction was the same. "They take me for a madman," Moche said to himself one day. "No one will believe me!"

Months later, Nazi storm troopers entered the little Hungarian town. They raided Jewish homes and made Elie and his Jewish neighbors wear yellow stars. Then, one day, an order was given that all Jews were to be moved from the town. Elie and his neighbors were marched down to the train station and herded into cattle cars. The doors were bolted. The train's whistle gave an eerie blast and its huge, iron wheels began to turn.

Shouting Woman

On the third night of travel, a woman in Elie's car began to shriek, "Fire! I can see fire!" Elie saw a woman pointing through an opening in the car into the night. Some men pushed her aside to have a look. But they saw nothing. The woman continued shouting, "Fire! I saw fire!"

"You saw nothing," the others said. "You were having a nightmare." But the woman kept shouting. Finally, to keep her quiet, a couple of young men forced her to the floor and gagged her.

A few hours later, the train slowed down. Elie cupped his hands around his eyes and peered out an opening in the car. He squinted and then squinted again. He couldn't believe what he was seeing. Outside were huge barbed-wire fences. In another few minutes the train came to a complete halt. Elie looked out again.

This time, he saw fire belching from a tall chimney from inside the fences. A terrible odor filled his nostrils. It was the smell of burning human flesh. The cattle cars, filled with Jews, had arrived at the reception center for the Auschwitz death camp.

Yancy closed the book and sat stunned. Then he looked out the plane window. Below, the beautiful countryside of the United States was rolling by—rivers with tug boats, fields of grain, and breathtaking mountains. Everything was so beautiful, so peaceful—and so far removed from anything like Auschwitz.

Yancey thought of something he had witnessed that morning in Philadelphia. A man was standing on a downtown street corner shouting to people on their way to work. He was warning that terrible things were going to happen. They had better be prepared. Nobody took the man seriously. Then Yancey thought about Moche and the shouting woman. No one had taken them seriously, either.

True Prophets?

What was Yancey trying to tell us through this story? Was he just sharing the thoughts that went on in his mind after reading a very moving book? I think he was doing this, and more. I think he was saying, also, that it's awfully hard, at times, to separate true warnings from false alarms. People in Elie's hometown thought Moche was spreading a false alarm, for everyone knew that even the Nazis wouldn't gun down crowds of innocent people! And the shouting woman on the train? Well, she was simply a very sick person who needed to be restrained for everyone's good.

As I thought about Moche and the shouting woman, I wondered about our own times. Who are the people today who are uttering true warnings? Who are the people who are spreading false alarms? In other words, who are the true prophets, and who are the false prophets?

For example, we hear people warning us about the need for nuclear restraint, respect for life, and protection of the environment. Are these people true prophets? Or are they false prophets? How do you tell a true prophet from a false prophet? How would you answer that question?

John

The story about Elie, Moche, and the shouting woman also reminded me of John the Baptist. Many people in biblical times looked upon John the way people in Elie's hometown looked upon Moche. Jesus testifies to this. In Luke 7, Jesus says to a group of hecklers:

"John the Baptist came, and he fasted and drank no wine, and you said, 'He has a demon in him!' The Son of Man came, and he ate and drank, and you said, 'Look at his man! He is a glutton and wine-drinker, a friend of tax collectors and other outcasts!'"

(Luke 7:33–34)

What was John the Baptist like? How did most people react to him? Let's take a closer look at these questions.

Not far from the Dead Sea there's a shallow spot in the Jordan River. As long as anyone could remember, it had been a favorite crossing for caravans, traders, and travelers from all over the Near East. It was a popular place for people to gather and exchange world news. This is the place where John showed up one day to preach and to baptize the people. He had an animal skin thrown around his gaunt, desert-hardened body. This gave him the appearance of a prophet of old.

In John's day, excitement and entertainment were not so easy to come by as they are today. And so, when the news spread that a strangely dressed man had come out of the desert and was preaching at the river, crowds flocked to hear what he had to say.

Call to Conversion

"Turn away from your sins and be baptized! Get the road ready for the Lord! The kingdom of heaven is near!" John shouted. "What sins are you talking about?" someone asked laughingly. "I don't see any kingdom coming!" shouted another. "The desert has baked his brain!" laughed another.

But there were others who took John's words more seriously. Deep down in their hearts, they knew that many things in their lives were far from what they should be. What John was saying made good sense. If God's Kingdom were actually coming, some big changes should be made.

John's expression "turn away from your sins" translates the Greek word *metanoia*. Recall that the gospels were originally written in Greek. *Metanoia* means a change in mind and heart. It means to bring one's personal viewpoints and attitudes more in line with what God wants them to be. The Hebrew word from which *metanoia* comes is even more colorful and graphic. It means to return from a wrong road and to set out, anew, on the right road.

John's Baptism

John's point is this. He is calling for a complete conversion, a total turnabout in one's thinking and acting. As a sign of sincerity that one wants to turn around, wash away the past and start out again clean and new, John tells the people to come into the water and be baptized. He warns them sternly, however, not to present themselves for baptism unless they are absolutely ready. He says, "Do those things that show that you have turned from your sins." (Luke 3:8)

Let me digress for a minute to illustrate by a very simple example the kind of sincere commitment that John was asking of people. In her book *Something More,* Catherine Marshall describes a turning point in the spiritual life of her daughter Linda.

One day, Linda was about to take a shower. She was standing with one foot in the shower stall and the other foot still on the bathroom rug. As she stood there momentarily, in this awkward position, it occurred to her that this was a perfect picture of her life. Often in the past she had been on the threshold of committing her life, once and for all, to Jesus. But she could never quite bring herself to take that final step. She always kept one foot in and one foot out.

It occurred to her then that the moment had finally come. She must decide for Jesus or against him. There was no longer any middle ground. She says, "Standing there, I carefully weighed what choosing the Lord's side would cost me. Obviously, some things in my life would have to go. But I was tired of living in two worlds and enjoying neither. Desperately, I longed for his peace in my heart. I took a deep breath and said aloud, 'I choose you, Lord.' Then I got in the shower. That shower was my true baptism."

This is kind of what John was asking the people

to do. He was asking them to take an honest look at their lives. Were they happy with what they saw? How happy? How unhappy? How might they change the things in their lives that made them unhappy? How could they begin to change, right now?

Repentance Sign

John's invitation to step into the water and be baptized was only for those who really wanted to change. It was a sign of their desire to turn back from traveling down a wrong road and setting out anew on the right road. It was only the first step in a journey. It was only a sign. It was only a start. John made this perfectly clear when he said:

"I baptize you with water to show that you have repented, but the one who will come after me will baptize you with the Holy Spirit and fire. He is much greater than I am; and I am not good enough even to carry his sandals."

(Matthew 3:11)

In other words, John is saying that his baptism is only a preparation for one to come. John's baptism is only a sign to show that the person wants to begin a new life. Jesus would baptize them with the Holy Spirit. It is the Holy Spirit who will bring them that new life. John's baptism is a baptism of repentance, rejecting one's former life. The baptism of Jesus is a baptism of rebirth, receiving a new life.

There's a fascinating episode in the Acts of the Apostles that underscores the point that John's baptism is merely a preparation for what we now call Christian baptism. The episode occurs in the ministry of the apostle Paul, which, of course, was a number of years after John's ministry at the Jordan. It took place right after Paul's arrival in the famous city of Ephesus.

There [Paul] found some disciples and asked them, "Did you receive the Holy Spirit when you became believers?" "We have not even heard that there is a Holy Spirit," they answered. "Well, then, what kind of baptism did you receive?" Paul asked. "The baptism of John," they answered. Paul said, "The baptism of John was for those who turned from their sins; and John told the people of Israel to believe in the one who was coming after him—that is, in Jesus." When the people heard this, they were baptized in the name of the Lord Jesus. Paul placed his hands on them, and the Holy Spirit came upon them.

(Acts 19:1-6)

Jesus' Baptism

Earlier, I used the story of Linda Marshall to illustrate the idea behind John's baptism—that it was only a sign of one's desire to change, nothing more. Let me use another story to illustrate the idea behind Christian baptism, that is, the receiving of a whole new life from the Holy Spirit. And that life is the very life of the risen Jesus.

The Norwegian anthropologist Thor Heyerdahl had a theory. He believed that ancient South Americans could have migrated 4,300 miles westward across the Pacific Ocean to Polynesia. Heyerdahl believed they could do this simply by letting ocean currents carry them on rafts to the Polynesian islands. Guided by ancient drawings, Heyerdahl built a man-made raft. He called it *Kon Tiki.*

While some people made fun of him, Heyerdahl proved his theory by floating his raft from South America to the Polynesian islands. That's a distance equivalent to that between Moscow and Chicago.

The amazing part of this story is that Heyerdahl once had a deathly fear of water. How could anybody with a fear of water attempt to cross 4,300 miles of ocean on a tiny raft? Well, something happened to Heyerdahl during World War II that removed that fear. He was training in Canada with free Norwegian forces. One day, as part of his training, he was put in a canoe on the Oxtongue River. In the middle of the river, the canoe capsized, throwing him head first into the roaring waters of the river. He struggled wildly as the waters engulfed him.

But soon he became exhausted, and he sank like a stone. As he did, a strange thought flashed through his mind. Heyerdahl's father was a Christian and believed in life after death. His mother had no religion and believed that death was the end of everything. The thought that flashed in Heyerdahl's mind was that he would soon learn which of his parents was right, his father or his mother.

Then, Heyerdahl says, the words of the Lord's prayer came to him and he began to pray them. As he did, a burst of energy surged through his body, and he began to battle the waters. Slowly, he overcame them and somehow survived the near tragedy. Heyerdahl was transformed by the experience. The fearful, old Heyerdahl died somewhere in the waters of the river and was buried there. And the new Heyerdahl was born in the same waters and rose from them. Something like this happens in baptism. Paul expresses it this way in Colossians 2:

When you were baptized, you were buried with Christ, and in baptism you were also raised with Christ. . . . You were at one time spiritually dead. . . . But God has now brought you to life with Christ.

(Colossians 2:12–13)

Rebirth Sign

To better appreciate Paul's image of baptism, we should keep in mind that Christians of his time were baptized by submersion. Many Christians today are still baptized by submersion. The whole body of the person is submerged under water. This explains why the places of baptism in early Christian churches were sunk into the floor. Three steps led down to them. The person being baptized was submerged, or buried, completely under the waters.

The baptistry acted, therefore, as a kind of tomb into which the person descended and was buried, and as a kind of womb from which the person emerged reborn in Christ. Tomb, death, burial. Womb, life, birth.

Paul says in Romans 6:

When we were baptized into union with Christ Jesus, we were baptized into union with his death. By our baptism we were buried with Christ and shared his death in order that just as Christ was raised from death . . . so also we might live a new life.

(Romans 6:3–4)

John Baptizes Jesus

Let's now return to the biblical scene of John baptizing in the Jordan River. John had been preaching and baptizing for several weeks. Then, one day, John was surprised by a sight that he hadn't anticipated. There, wading through the waters to be baptized, was Jesus.

John was caught completely off guard. He just stood there, wondering what to do or what to say. Here's how Matthew describes what happened next:

> John tried to make Jesus change his mind. "I ought to be baptized by you," he said, "and yet you have come to me!" But Jesus answered him, "Let it be so for now."
>
> (Matthew 3:14-15)

Why did Jesus present himself for baptism? After all, he had never sinned! He had no need to repent. He had never given in to evil. The gospel writers never really answer this question. Many Christians, however, regard this action of Jesus as a sign of his desire to identify himself with us completely. Jesus was tempted as we are, and he understood the powerful attraction of evil. Because Jesus experienced this powerful attraction to evil himself, he understood sinners. When Jesus allowed John to baptize him, Jesus was really identifying with us as sinners.

Luke describes the baptism of Jesus this way:

> After all the people had been baptized, Jesus also was baptized. While he was praying, heaven was opened, and the Holy Spirit came down upon him in bodily form like a dove. And a voice came

from heaven, *"You are my own dear Son. I am
pleased with you."*

(Luke 3:21-22)

New Era

Three things stand out in this remarkable scene.
First, the sky opens above Jesus standing there in
the water. This unusual image of the sky opening
recalls the prayer of Isaiah, where the prophet
pleads with God to "tear open the sky" and come
down and set things right on Earth. The psalmist
also employs this same image for the same reason.

New Creation

The second thing to remember about this scene
is that after the opening of the sky, the spirit of
God descends in a dovelike form. The image of
the dovelike form hovering over Jesus in the water
brings to mind the story of creation. In Genesis,
the Spirit of God is portrayed as hovering over the
waters. Luke's use of this image suggests that the
baptism of Jesus is the signal for the start of a
whole new creation. Just as the power of God
hovered over the waters at the dawn of the creation, so now the Spirit of God hovers over Jesus
standing in the waters. A new creation is beginning! A new day is dawning!

New Adam

The third thing to note is the voice coming
from heaven and saying, "You are my own dear
Son. I am pleased with you." These words had a
profound significance for the Jews. They echo the
very wording and spirit of two important Old Testament prophesies. The psalmist set to music the
first prophecy in Psalm 2, "You are my son; today

I have become your father . . . the whole earth will be yours."

The second prophecy speaks of the coming of a suffering hero. The prophet Isaiah has God say of this hero, "Here is my servant . . . with whom I am pleased. I have filled him with my spirit, and he will bring justice to every nation."

So, then, three striking images mark the baptism of Jesus. First, the sky opens. Second, a dovelike form descends. Third, a voice from heaven speaks. The open sky is a sign that a "new era" in human history begins with the baptism of Jesus. The dovelike form is a sign that this new era consists of a new creation, or re-creation, of the world. The voice from heaven indicates that Jesus is the "new Adam," God's firstborn son of the new creation. Speaking of Jesus as the "new Adam," Paul says:

The first man, Adam, was created a living being; but the last Adam [Jesus] is the life-giving spirit. . . . The first Adam, made of earth, came from the earth; the second Adam [Jesus] came from heaven. . . . Just as we wear the likeness of the man made of earth [the first Adam], so we will wear the likeness of the man from heaven [Jesus, the second Adam].

(1 Corinthians 15:45–49)

History Turns a Corner

And so, John's appearance at the Jordan River set in motion a series of important events, events that would change the course of history. Like many prophets before him, John was misunderstood by many people. Some even ridiculed him. But some took his words seriously. John invited people to "turn away from their sins" in preparation for the arrival of God's Kingdom, the "new era" foretold by the prophets. As a sign of their repentance, John instructed the people to receive a baptism of repentance. It showed the people's desire to reject the sinfulness of their old lives.

John made it clear to the people, however, that his baptism was merely in preparation for one that was to come, the baptism prescribed by Jesus. This baptism would be a baptism of rebirth. It would communicate to those who received it a whole new life, the very life of the risen Jesus.

Finally, the day came when Jesus presented himself for baptism. The baptism Jesus received was a baptism of revelation. It revealed that God was beginning the new era in human history. It was the new era foretold by the prophets. The new era would take the form of a new creation. Jesus himself was the new Adam of this new creation.

Let me close, now, with what television people sometimes call a tight focus. It is on Jesus and John. Their lives were closely interwoven and, as you might expect, they admired, respected, and loved one another deeply. One day, Jesus spoke about his feelings for his friend. He said to a group of people:

"When you went out to John in the desert, what did you expect to see? A blade of grass bending in the wind? What did you go out to see? A man dressed up in fancy clothes? Tell me, what did you go out to see? A prophet! Yes, indeed, but you saw much more than a prophet."

(Luke 7:24–26)

MEDITATION/DISCUSSION POINTS

1. The author says, "As I thought about Moche and the shouting woman, I wondered about our own times. . . . We hear people warning us about the need for nuclear restraint, respect for life, and protection of the environment. Are these people true prophets?" How do you tell a true prophet from a false prophet?

2. The book says: "John's expression 'turn away from your sins' translates the Greek work *metanoia,* which means a change in mind and heart." Recall a change in mind and heart that you have experienced in your life.

3. Recall a time when you experienced a true "moment of decision" similar to the one Linda Marshall experienced in the shower.

4. What was your closest brush with death? Did it change you in any way, as Heyerdahl's near tragedy changed him?

5. The book says: "Why did Jesus present himself for baptism? After all, he had never sinned! . . . The gospel writers never really answer this question." What explanation might you suggest for this?

We have a High Priest who was tempted in every way that we are, but did not sin. Let us be brave, then, and approach God's throne, where there is grace. There we will receive mercy and find grace to help us just when we need it. *Hebrews 4:15–16*

7. INTO THE DESERT WITH JESUS

There's a strange fascination about putting everything you need to survive on your back and taking off alone. You head down some wilderness trail for an afternoon, a day, or even a week. Why are people, especially young people, drawn to this kind of an adventure? Have you ever felt the urge to get away yourself? I know I certainly have.

In an article in *Campus Life,* Doug Alderson tells why he took off on a summer-long 2,000-mile hike down the Appalachian Trail. "I had just graduated from high school. I had many questions. My goals in life? My future? Was there a God? I thought the answers might lie in the beautiful wilderness ahead. There had to be more to life than money, TV, parties and getting high. In a sense, my hike was a search for inner peace, a journey to find myself."

Chance to Think

Doug said the long hours of solitude along the trail gave him a chance to think back across his life and plan ahead for the future. They gave him a chance to know himself better because there was no one around to influence him.

But it wasn't all joy and discovery for Doug. There were times when he wondered whether he had bitten off more than he could chew. Some mountainous parts of the trail were steep and hard to climb. There were also times when Doug wondered whether all the pain was worth the effort. There were chilly days when it rained. His clothes got soaked, his feet were wet, and his whole body shivered and ached. There were times when he was lonely and tired and had no one to turn to for comfort.

But Doug stuck it out. Five months later he returned home a changed person. Even his dog eyed him strangely when he walked into the house, as if to say, "Where have you been? What have you done? You look different." Doug was different. He found what he was searching for, "peace from within, and peace from God."

Doug summed up his experience this way, "I was more my own person. I liked what I saw in myself."

Jesus Alone

Doug Alderson belongs to that long line of people in history who have gone off alone for a period of time to take inventory of themselves and to ask questions about the meaning of life. Moses did it. The prophets did it. John the Baptist did it.

It comes as no surprise, therefore, to find that Jesus, too, did it.

[After Jesus was baptized] the Spirit led him into the desert. . . . After spending forty days and nights without food, Jesus was hungry. Then the Devil came to him and said, "If you are God's Son, order these stones to turn into bread." But Jesus answered, "The scripture says, 'Man cannot live on bread alone, but needs every word that God speaks.'" Then the Devil took Jesus to Jerusalem, the Holy City, set him on the highest point of the Temple, and said to him, "If you are God's Son, throw yourself down, for the scripture says, 'God will give orders to his angels about you; they will hold you up with their hands, so that not even your feet will be hurt on the stones.'" Jesus answered, "But the scripture also says, 'Do not put the Lord

your God to the test.'" Then the Devil took Jesus to a very high mountain and showed him all the kingdoms of the world in all their greatness. "All this I will give you," the Devil said, "if you kneel down and worship me." Then Jesus answered, "Go away, Satan! The scripture says, 'Worship the Lord your God and serve only him!'" Then the Devil left Jesus.

(Matthew 4:1–11)

Years ago, a British television team went to the Holy Land to make a movie of the life of Jesus. They ran into trouble when it came to filming the temptations of Jesus. The big problem was how to portray the devil. Many ancient artists portrayed the devil in an incredible way. They showed him with an ugly body, a tail, and horns. Modern arists prefer to show the devil in a more realistic way. For example, they might give him a business suit, a brief case, and a pair of glasses.

How would you show Satan in a TV production? The British television team eventually decided to portray the devil by simply showing a shadow on the sand.

This solution seemed to work. It avoided useless argument about how Jesus experienced the devil. Was the devil present in the mind of Jesus? Or was the devil present in a physical way? That is, did the devil approach Jesus the way I'd approach you on the street? The British television team decided to place the focus on Jesus, not on the devil.

Gospel Preview

That brings us to the three temptations of Jesus. If you're like me, you enjoy watching movie previews. A good preview gives you the spirit of the movie without spoiling it. You see just enough of the action to get you interested, but not enough to spoil the plot. The temptations of Jesus are something like that. They act as a kind of preview of the gospel story.

Who Is Jesus?

For example, they hint at the answer the gospel will give to two important questions about Jesus. The first question is, "Who is Jesus?" There's a story that's told about an old German philosopher. One day he was walking down the street, deep in thought. Absentmindedly, he bumped right into a woman. The woman was furious! When she recovered her balance, she yelled, "Well, who do you think you are?" The philosopher looked at her in a confused way and said, "Madam, how I wish I knew! How I wish I knew!"

There are times in all of our lives when we're not quite sure who we are. Sometimes we do things that make us feel good, and we think we are good. But there are other times when we do things that make us feel ashamed, and we wonder how good we really are. I know I went through this experience when I was a boy. Then, when I got older, I discovered that most people wonder about themselves in this way.

There's an old poem about a soldier about to enter battle. He was thinking about life and about himself. His thoughts went something like this:

My chaplain says I'm a sinner.
My country says I'm a saint.
But both of them are wrong.
For I'm neither of them, I ain't.
I'm a human being. That's what I am.

There's part of me that's good,
and part of me that's bad.
There's nothing in me that's perfect,
and nothing in me that's complete.
I'm nothing but a great beginning,
from the top of my head,
to the soles of my feet.

That poem, which I have recreated here from memory, really impressed me. It says simply that I'm a human being. This means I'm not perfect; I'm not complete. There are moments when I act like a saint, and there are other moments I'd rather not talk about.

But let's get back to Jesus. The desert story leaves no doubt about Jesus. It shows that he is human, just like you and me. Jesus experienced temptation, just as we do. The way Jesus responded to temptation, however, shows something else. It shows that Jesus is also totally different from us. Although he was tempted like us, he did not fall.

No human being ever showed such power over the devil as did Jesus. No human being ever showed such firmness in the face of temptation. The way Jesus responded to temptation shows that he is far more than just another human being. There is something about Jesus that surpasses ordinary human nature.

What is that something? The devil himself suggests the answer. Before each temptation he says to Jesus, "If you are the Son of God." Jesus is not just another human being. Jesus is the very Son of God become man. Years later, Paul would describe Jesus this way in Philippians 2: "He always had the nature of God, but he . . . took the nature of a servant. He became like man."

How Jesus took the nature of man but retained the nature of God is something we will never understand in this life. But he did do it. And so we may answer the first question by writing "man and God."

Why Did Jesus Come?

Besides previewing the answer to the question "Who is Jesus?" the temptations of Jesus also preview the answer to the question "Why did Jesus come into the world?" To help us find the answer to this question, let's go back to the baptism of Jesus.

Jesus . . . came to John at the Jordan to be baptized by him. But John tried to make him change his mind. "I ought to be baptized by you," John said, "and yet you have come to me!" But Jesus answered him, "Let it be so for now. For in this way we shall do all that God requires." So John agreed. As soon as Jesus was baptized, he came up out of the water. Then heaven was opened to him, and he saw the Spirit of God coming down like a dove and lighting on him. Then a voice said from heaven, "This is my own dear Son, with whom I am pleased."

(Matthew 3:13-17)

So, following the baptism of Jesus, three things happened. First, the sky opened. Next, a dovelike form descended upon Jesus. Third, a voice called out, "This is my own dear Son, with whom I am pleased." The open sky calls to mind the prayer of Isaiah. He pleaded with God to tear open the sky, come down, and set things right on earth. In other words, he pleaded with God to establish a new era on earth, that is, the promised Kingdom of God. The open sky suggests this is now happening.

The dove, or Spirit of God, hovering over Jesus in the waters of the Jordan recalls the power of God hovering over the waters of creation. It suggests that the new era, God's Kingdom on earth, will be a whole new creation or re-creation of the world.

The voice from heaven saying "This is my own dear Son" suggests that Jesus is the new Adam, the firstborn person of the new creation.

Now we can see how significantly the devil's temptation of Jesus fits in. Just as the first or "old Adam" was tempted by the devil right after God's first creation, so Jesus, the "new Adam," was tempted by the devil right after the new creation.

The first Adam gave in to temptation; Jesus, the "new Adam," did not. This suggests the answer to our second question, "Why did Jesus come?" Jesus is the "new Adam." He came to right the wrongs of the 'old' Adam. The first Adam fell to the power of evil; Jesus, the second Adam, did not.

By reversing this situation, Jesus brings new life into the world. By turning the tables on the devil, Jesus brings new hope into the world. Years afterward, Paul would write:

Just as all people die because of their union with [the first] Adam, in the same way all will be raised to life because of their union with Christ [the second Adam]. . . . The first Adam . . . came from the earth; the second Adam [Jesus] came from heaven. . . . Just as we wear the likeness of [the first Adam], the man made of earth, so we will

wear the likeness of [Jesus, the second Adam]
the Man from heaven.

(1 Corinthians 15:22, 47-49)

So we have the answer to our second question, why Jesus came into the world. Jesus came to be the "new Adam." He came to right the wrongs of the first Adam.

How Jesus Will Do It

The reaction of Jesus to the three temptations of Satan previews yet another dimension of the person of Jesus. It gives us our first idea of how Jesus will accomplish his work on earth. How does the reaction of Jesus to the temptations of Satan do this? Take the first temptation.

Then the Devil came to Jesus and said, "If you are God's Son, order these stones to turn into bread."

(Matthew 4:3)

By Suffering

Jesus rejected the devil's suggestions. By refusing to turn stones into bread, Jesus shows that he will not use his extraordinary powers to escape pain. He will not protect himself from suffering. He will leave himself vulnerable to pain and suffering, just as you and I are.

In other words, Jesus will work, sweat, go hungry, and suffer to accomplish his work on earth, just as you and I must. Suffering is the first way Jesus will accomplish his work on earth.

By Serving

Now take the second temptation of Jesus:

Then the Devil took Jesus to Jerusalem, the Holy City, set him on the highest point of the

Temple, and said to him, "If you are God's Son, throw yourself down, for the scripture says, 'God will give orders to his angels about you; they will hold you up with their hands, so that not even your feet will be hurt on the stones.'"

(Matthew 4:5-6)

Again, the devil tried to get Jesus to misuse powers. But Jesus refused. Jesus did not yield to the temptation. By refusing the help of angels, by refusing to allow them to serve him, Jesus makes an important point. He shows that he has come on earth not to be served but to serve. Later he would instruct his disciples, "If one of you wants to be great, he must be the servant of the rest. . . . Even the Son of Man did not come to be served; he came to serve." Serving is the second way Jesus will accomplish his mission on earth.

If we Christians would have the courage to follow the example of Jesus and place ourselves at the service of others, we would be happier people, and this world would be a happier place.

A Lesson for Me

This point was brought home to me forcefully a few months back. I was boarding a plane back to Chicago. I had just given a retreat to some inmates and staff members of a federal prison. When I got on the plane, it was nearly empty. I was tired, so I picked a row of seats and settled down for some sleep.

I had just taken my shoes off when a teenage girl came stumbling down the aisle. She was really a sight. She was dressed in a tee shirt and jeans. A backpack dangled from her shoulder.

Under one arm she carried a magazine and a tennis racket. Under the other arm she carried a beat-up shopping bag stuffed with clothes. And now for the incredible part. Would you believe it? She walked right past all those rows of empty seats to where I sat. She looked straight at me and said, "Hi!"

"Oh, no!" I said to myself as I returned her greeting. With that she passed me her backpack, then her tennis racket, then her shopping bag. Then she followed.

There I was wedged into a single seat, with my suitcase under my feet and her tennis racket, her backpack, and her beat-up shopping bag stacked around me. Then she came in.

She began to talk. She had just been ordered onto the plane by her mother, who no longer wanted her around. Now she was on her way to stay with her father. She told me that everything in her life was beginning to fall apart. She couldn't get along with her mother. Her brother took her mother's side. Her boyfriends were turning out to be creeps. Even her best friend had just betrayed her. Finally, she wasn't looking forward to living with her father.

Then, after about twenty minutes of nonstop talking she paused and said pathetically, "Father, what should I do?" If she would have asked me that question twenty minutes earlier, I would have known exactly what to say, "Move five rows forward!" But now, I could see how much anger and pain she was carrying around inside her.

I turned to her and said, "Karen, I really can't tell you what to do. But I can tell you a story about a girl named Connie who was in a situation much like yours. Connie went to a counselor for help. After she had told him everything, he took her hand gently and said, 'Here's what I want you to do. I want you to volunteer your services to help some people who can no longer help themselves. A hospital for the severely handicapped or a nursing home for the very elderly would be ideal. Do you know of any such places?' "

" 'Yes,' she said with a surprised look. The counselor then continued. 'I want you to spend a few hours a week helping these people in whatever way you can. Bathe them, help them to the bathroom, wash their hair, read to them, write letters for them, or just hold their hands. Do you think you can do that?' The girl sat stunned for a moment. Then she said, 'I think I can.' The counselor rose to his feet and said, 'Good! I'll see you in six weeks.'

"Six weeks later, the girl returned. She was bubbling over with excitement. 'You won't believe what's happened,' she said. 'I've just had the best six weeks of my life. I never knew people could be so nice.' "

Back on the plane Karen looked at me and said, "Father, you don't have to finish the story. I see what you mean." We talked the rest of the way to Chicago about life and the meaning of life. When our plane touched down at O'Hare, Karen turned and said to me, "Father, you've helped me more than you'll ever know." Suddenly I didn't feel tired anymore. Thanks to what Karen had just said, I felt great. It's funny. I started out helping Karen. She ended up helping me. I guess that's what serving other people is really all about.

By Not Compromising

This brings us to the third temptation.

Then the Devil took Jesus to a very high mountain and showed him all the kingdoms of the world in all their greatness. "All this I will give you," the Devil said, "if you kneel down and worship me."
(Matthew 4:8–9)

Personally, I have always found this temptation difficult to understand. At first glance it seems so gross, so obviously wrong. Then one day someone gave me a new way to look at the temptation. The person said, "I think the devil was merely saying something like this to Jesus: 'Think of all the poor people in the world. Think of all the exploited people in the world. Think of all the suffering people in the world. They await your coming with tears. They cry out for your help with open hands. But unless you have power, you won't be able to help them. Let me share my power with you. Let me help you to help them. Together, we will take away all their pain. Together, we will wipe away all their tears.' But Jesus would not listen to Satan's insincere offer. He turned a deaf ear to Satan's invitation."

By refusing to bow to Satan, Jesus shows that he will never compromise with evil in any form, for any reason, no matter how good or how noble it may seem. And so Jesus accomplishes his work on earth by not compromising.

When I think of compromise, I think of Robert Bolt's play, *A Man for All Seasons*. In this true story, Lord Norfolk tries to persuade his friend Sir Thomas More to sign a document. The document states that he thinks the marriage of King Henry

VIII is lawful. If More refuses to sign the document, Henry will execute him for treason.

More does not believe the marriage is lawful, and he refuses to compromise his conscience and sign the document. Lord Norfolk grows impatient with Sir Thomas and says to his friend, "Oh, confound all this. . . . Frankly I don't know whether the marriage is lawful or not. But damn it, Thomas, look at these names. . . . You know these men! Can't you do what I did and come with us, for fellowship?"

Sir Thomas still refuses. He will not compromise his conscience, whether it be for his King, for his friends, or to save his own life. He was later executed.

Preview

So the reaction of Jesus to the devil's temptations gives us a preview of three important things about Jesus. First, it tells us who Jesus is. He is the very Son of God become man. Second, it tells us why Jesus came into the world. Jesus is the "new Adam," who came into the world to restore life and hope to people.

Finally, the reaction of Jesus gives us an insight into how Jesus will accomplish his work. First, he will suffer. He will even die to accomplish his work. Second, he will serve others and not place himself above or before them. Finally, Jesus will never compromise with evil under any form or for any reason.

Let me conclude with the prayer of Saint Francis. It summarizes many of the points we have been making:

"Lord, make me an instrument of your peace.

Where there is hatred let me sow love; where there is injury, pardon; where there is doubt, faith; where there is despair, hope; where there is darkness, light; and where there is sadness, joy. Grant that I may not so much seek to be consoled as to console; to be understood as to understand; to be loved as to love. For it is in giving that we receive; it is in pardoning that we are pardoned; and it is in dying that we are born to eternal life."

MEDITATION/DISCUSSION POINTS

1. Recall a "desert experience" (a time when you were pretty much alone) that helped you see things in a new light—as Doug Alderson saw them after his hike.

2. The author says, "By refusing to turn stones into bread, Jesus shows that he will not use his extraordinary powers to escape pain." Recall a time when some person voluntarily underwent pain to help you or someone close to you.

3. The book says, "The temptations of Jesus . . . act as a kind of preview of the gospel." Review how they do this. How do Jesus' temptations make him more approachable and more appealing to you personally?

4. "It's funny," says the author. "I started out helping Karen. She ended up helping me. I guess that is what serving other people is all about." Recall a time when some similar experience happened to you.

5. Recall a time when, like Thomas More, you were put under considerable pressure to compromise your principles or your conscience. What helped you most at this time to do what was right?

"Go back and tell John what you have seen and heard: the blind can see, the lame can walk . . . the deaf can hear, the dead are raised to life, and the Good News is preached to the poor. How happy are those who have no doubts about me!" *Luke 7:22–23*

8. MIRACLES OF JESUS

The movie *E.T.* broke box-office records across the country. One of the fun things about the movie is the way the little extraterrestrial tried to learn about everything here on earth. The things you and I take for granted amazed E.T.

Let's play a little game. Suppose you and E.T. were walking down the street. Suddenly E.T. stops. He points to two men, a big man and a little man, walking slowly around a car. E.T. jumps nervously when the big man kicks one of the rear tires of the car. He watches carefully as the little man lifts the hood of the car and shows the big man what lies inside.

E.T. puts his hands on his ears when the big man opens and slams all four car doors. Then the two men shake hands and disappear behind a door marked "Office."

"What was that all about?" asks E.T. "And why did they end by putting their hands together?" You smile and say, "It's all very simple, E.T. The little man was trying to sell the big man the car. Putting their hands together was a sign that they had come to an agreement and the sale was made." E.T. is satisfied and the two of you continue your walk.

Suddenly E.T. stops again. This time he is genuinely frightened. He points to a young man who has just leaped from a bus and is running at top speed down the street. Racing toward the young man is a young woman. When they meet, they embrace and just stand there motionless. E.T. points to drops of water falling from their eyes and rolling down their cheeks. "Why are those two people holding each other like that?" he asks. "And why is water coming from their eyes?"

You smile and say, "It's all right, E.T.! Don't worry. Holding each other like that is called hugging. It's a sign that two people like each other very much. The drops of water coming from their eyes are called tears. They are signs that the two people are very happy." E.T. gives a big sigh of relief, and the two of you continue your walk.

What was the point of our little game? It was to illustrate an important fact. If you hadn't been available to explain to E.T. the meaning of a handshake and a hug, he would not have understood their significance.

Many of our everyday actions are like the hug and the handshake. There is the action itself, and then there is the meaning of the action. For example, we hug someone, we wink at someone, we smile at someone. This is called body language. It shows how we feel toward a person. You and I take these signs for granted. But they would be confusing to someone from a completely different culture. Many actions in the life of Jesus were signs too. These signs also had deeper meanings.

Two Levels

Take the miracles of Jesus. Like the hug and the handshake, the miracles of Jesus had a deeper meaning. In other words, they operated at two levels. First, there was the sense level. That's what everybody saw: a blind person began to see again, a deaf person began to hear again, a lame person began to walk again. The sign level was the deeper meaning behind the action. It was what Jesus intended to say to people then and now.

So we have two levels: sense level, what people saw, and sign level, what Jesus meant or intended to say to us through the miracle.

Healing Miracles

Let's now take a closer look at the miracles of Jesus to try to determine what Jesus intended to teach through them. Let's begin with the healing miracles. There's a remarkable story about a concert pianist, Marta-Korwin Rhodes. She was in Warsaw when the city was attacked during World War II. Instead of fleeing, she remained behind to help the wounded in the crowded hospitals.

One night, as she was walking through the wards, she came upon a young soldier sobbing loudly. This sight moved her deeply. What could she do to help this young man? She looked at her hands. If these hands could create harmony from a piano, why couldn't they create harmony directly? She placed her hands on the young man's head, and prayed, "O God, help this young man. He's in misery and pain. Give him some of your love and your peace. Comfort him in his moment of trial." Almost immediately, the soldier stopped sobbing and fell asleep.

What produced the remarkable change in the young man? What made him stop crying and fall asleep? Was it a coincidence? Was it a touch of the woman's hands that told him somebody cared about him? Was it God's grace that came as the result of the woman's prayer? Or was it a combination of all these? Jesus often used a combination of touch and prayer to heal people.

Once Jesus was in a town where there was a man who was suffering from a dreaded skin

119

disease. When he saw Jesus, he threw himself down and begged him, "Sir, if you want to, you can make me clean!" Jesus reached out and touched him. "I do want to," he answered. "Be clean!" At once the disease left the man.

(Luke 5:12–13)

Why Jesus Healed

Why did Jesus perform healing miracles like this? Was it because people begged him for healing? Was it because Jesus felt sorry for people? Or was there yet another reason? Certainly Jesus healed people because they asked him for healing, and certainly he healed people because his heart was moved to compassion for them.

But there was, indeed, another reason why Jesus performed healing miracles. The prophets had foretold that the coming of God's Kingdom would be accompanied by certain signs. The prophet Isaiah spoke of God's intervention in human history this way:

Tell everyone who is discouraged, "Be strong and don't be afraid! God is coming to your rescue. . . ." The blind will be able to see, and the deaf will hear. The lame will leap and dance, and those who cannot speak will shout for joy.

(Isaiah 35:4–6)

This is what Jesus made happen by his miracles. When John the Baptist sent his disciples to ask Jesus if he were the promised one who would inaugurate the Kingdom of God, Jesus said:

"Tell John what you have seen and heard: the blind can see, the lame can walk . . . the deaf can

120

hear, the dead are raised to life, and the Good
News is preached to the poor."

(Luke 7:22)

By his miracles, Jesus is fulfilling the signs foretold by Isaiah. He is inaugurating the Kingdom of God on earth. The healing miracles of Jesus are signs announcing to the people that the long-awaited Kingdom of God is at hand.

Expelling Demons

Besides healing people of all kinds of ailments and diseases, Jesus worked other kinds of miracles. For example, he expelled demons from people. That is, he freed people from evil spirits.

A few years ago there were a lot of novels and films dealing with people who were possessed by an evil spirit. The most famous of these was *The Exorcist,* by William Blatty. It concerned a young person who was possessed by an evil power. The novel was based on a true case of a fourteen-year-old boy who lived in Mount Rainier, Maryland, in 1949.

At night, furniture in the boy's room slammed about. He could hardly sleep. Later, when taken to a university hospital, even stranger things happened. The boy grew violent. He spoke ancient languages. And once, while helplessly strapped in bed, he had long red scratches appear on his body. Eventually the boy was exorcised, and he now lives a normal life in the Washington, D.C., area.

I knew one of the priests involved in that exorcism. He would never talk about it in detail, except to say that the episode had a profound effect upon his life.

The gospel portrays Jesus as involving himself frequently in cases like this. Listen to this extraordinary story:

Jesus and his disciples arrived on the other side of Lake Galilee, in the territory of Gerasa. As soon as Jesus got out of the boat, he was met by a man who came out of the burial caves there. This man had an evil spirit in him and lived among the tombs. Nobody could keep him tied with chains any more; many times his feet and his hands had been tied, but every time he broke the chains and smashed the irons on his feet. He was too strong for anyone to control. Day and night he wandered among the tombs and through the hills, screaming and cutting himself with stones. He was some distance away when he saw Jesus; so he ran, fell on his knees before him, and screamed in a loud voice, "Jesus, Son of the Most High God! What do you want with me? For God's sake, I beg you, don't punish me!" (He said this because Jesus was saying, "Evil spirit, come out of this man!") [With that the evil spirit left the man.] . . . People went out to see what had happened, and when they came to Jesus, they saw the man . . . sitting there, clothed and in his right mind; and they were all afraid. . . . The man left and went all through the Ten Towns, telling what Jesus had done for him. And all who heard it were amazed.

(Mark 5:1–8, 14–15, 20)

Why Jesus Expelled Demons

What was the deeper meaning behind this action of Jesus? What was it a sign of? What was Jesus trying to say by expelling evil spirits from people? Jesus answered this question himself one day after he had expelled an evil spirit.

The crowds were amazed, but some of the people said, "It is Beelzebul, the chief of the demons, who gives him the power to drive them out."... But Jesus knew what they were thinking, so he said to them, "Any country that divides itself into groups which fight each other will not last very long.... You say that I drive out demons because Beelzebul gives me the power to do so.... No, it is rather by means of God's power that I drive out demons, and this proves that the Kingdom of God has already come to you."

(Luke 11:14–20)

And so Jesus presents his power over evil spirits as a sign that the Kingdom of God has indeed come. Jesus is saying through his action of exorcism, "The Kingdom of Satan is ending; the Kingdom of God is beginning."

Nature Miracles

Besides healing people, and besides expelling evil spirits from people, Jesus also showed mastery over nature. I came to respect the power of nature during World War II. One time I spent twenty-two days crossing the Pacific Ocean on a tiny Liberty ship. We were following a zigzag course to avoid detection by Japanese submarines. On stormy nights the ocean lifted up tons of water and sent them crashing onto the ship's deck. The entire ship seemed to stagger in the water.

This was a frightening experience for me. I had never sailed on the ocean before. In the face of such awesome power in nature, I felt small and insignificant. Yet Jesus demonstrated complete mastery over such awesome power as this. One night Jesus was crossing the Sea of Galilee with some of his disciples.

Suddenly a strong wind blew up, and the waves began to spill over into the boat, so that it was about to fill with water. Jesus was in the back of the boat, sleeping with his head on a pillow. The disciples woke him up and said, "Teacher, don't you care that we are about to die?" Jesus stood up and commanded the wind, "Be quiet!" and he said to the waves, "Be still!" The wind died down, and there was a great calm. Then Jesus said to his disciples, "Why are you frightened? Do you still have no faith?" But they were terribly afraid and began to say to one another, "Who is this man? Even the wind and the waves obey him!"

(Mark 4:37–41)

Why Jesus Stilled the Storm

What was Jesus trying to say to his disciples by calming the storm on the Sea of Galilee? What deeper meaning did Jesus intend to communicate by this miracle? The answer is in the Old Testament. Psalm 107 praises God's power over nature in these words:

Some sailed over the ocean in ships. . . . They saw what the LORD can do, his wonderful acts on the seas. He commanded, and a mighty wind began to blow and stirred up the waves. The ships were lifted high in the air and plunged down into the depths. In such danger the men lost their courage; they stumbled and staggered like drunks—all their skill was useless. Then in their trouble they called to the LORD, and he saved them from their distress. He calmed the raging storm, and the waves became quiet.

(Psalm 107:23–29)

When Jesus calmed the storm at sea, he showed the same mastery over the force of nature that God showed in Old Testament times. Some scholars suggest that the power of Jesus over the storm is also another sign of his power over demons. Many ancients looked upon the sea as the abode or dwelling place of demons. So in stilling the storm, Jesus again demonstrated mastery over the forces of evil.

Kingdom Signs

The miracles of Jesus are awesome signs that the power of God is present in the person of Jesus. And Jesus used this power to save people from the forces of evil that have terrorized them and enslaved them for so long.

The miracles of Jesus are signs. They announce the arrival of God's Kingdom. The saving power of God is now at work in the world in the person of Jesus. Jesus is the promised Savior of Israel.

Conversion Signs

There is a second message that Jesus communicated through his miracles. In addition to announcing the arrival of God's Kingdom, the miracles of Jesus serve also as signs inviting people to turn from their sins and be converted, to open their hearts to the Kingdom.

Father Malachy's Miracle is a funny story. It is about a priest in Scotland who gets the idea of praying for a miracle. This miracle will be so spectacular that it will leave no doubt about God and religion.

The miracle he chooses, and here's the funny part, is to have the scandalous nightclub near his church lifted off its foundation and transported to a deserted island off the coast of Scotland. The next night Father Malachy kneels in prayer. At that very moment, the nightclub begins to rise up. It soars through the air and finally comes to rest on the island.

After the spectacular miracle, Father Malachy waits for newspaper headlines and crowds of people inquiring about God. But the very opposite happens. The owners of the nightclub turn the whole thing into a publicity stunt. A defeated Father Malachy returns to his knees and asks God to put an end to the whole affair. Suddenly the nightclub goes airborne and comes to rest, once again, in the shadow of Father Malachy's church. A wiser Father Malachy now realizes how foolish it was to think that a miracle was all that was needed to bring people to belief.

Father Malachy's Miracle makes an important point. It is the same one that John makes in his gospel. One day Jesus was walking along with his disciples. They came upon a blind man.

His disciples asked him, "Teacher, whose sin caused him to be born blind? Was it his own or his parents' sin?" Jesus answered, "His blindness has nothing to do with his sins or his parents' sins. He is blind so that God's power might be seen at work in him. As long as it is day, we must do the work of him who sent me; night is coming when no one can work. While I am in the world, I am the light for the world." After he said this, Jesus spat on the ground and made some mud with the spittle; he rubbed the mud on the man's eyes and told him, "Go and wash your face in the Pool of

Siloam." . . . So the man went, washed his face, and came back seeing.

(John 9:2–7)

The Jewish authorities, however, refused to believe that the man had been blind and had been healed.

Jesus said, "I came to this world to judge, so that the blind should see and those who see should become blind." Some Pharisees who were there with him heard him say this and asked him, "Surely you don't mean that we are blind, too?"

(John 9:39–40)

In other words, some of the Pharisees refused to believe. They closed their eyes to both the miracle itself and its deeper meaning. It is impossible to force another person to believe. Not even Jesus could do it, or wanted to do it.

Believing involves more than hearing words or seeing signs. It involves opening your mind and heart to what you see and hear. It involves being ready to view the world in a new way. It involves opening your eyes to a new level of reality. To those who close their minds and ears and eyes to his miracles, Jesus repeats the words of the prophet Isaiah:

"Their minds are dull, and they have stopped up their ears and have closed their eyes. Otherwise, their eyes would see, their ears would hear, their minds would understand, and they would turn to me, says God, and I would heal them."

(Matthew 13:15)

Invitations to Be Miracle Workers

And so, the miracles of Jesus were signs inviting people to open their hearts to God's Kingdom. Let me try to put it in another way. Jesus opened the eyes of the blind. But this miracle has a deeper meaning. It is a sign for us to open our eyes to the bright light of a new day that dawned with Jesus.

Jesus unplugged the ears of the deaf. And this miracle also has a deeper meaning. It is a sign for all of us to open our ears to what Jesus has to say.

Jesus raised the dead. Again, this miracle has a deeper meaning. It is a sign for us to be reborn, to begin living new lives in God's Kingdom here and now.

And many people did believe in Jesus. They turned from their sins and began to live new lives. They began to reach out to those in need. They gave hope and support to those who were discouraged. Everywhere they reached out, and everywhere they preached, things began to happen. Situations began to change before their eyes. People began to hope again. The words of Jesus began to come alive: "I was hungry and you fed me, thirsty and you gave me a drink; I was a stranger and you received me. . . . Whenever you did this for the least of these . . . you did it for me."

The followers of Jesus became miracle workers, like Jesus their master. They transformed the world of their day. They lived up to what Jesus had said of them.

"You are like salt for all mankind. . . . You are like light for the whole world. . . . Your light must

shine before people, so that they will see the good things you do and praise your Father in heaven."
(Matthew 5:13-16)

Two thousand years have passed into history since Jesus first spoke those words. But something has not passed. It is this. Jesus wants us, you and me, today, to take his words seriously. Jesus wants us to become miracle workers ourselves. He wants us to transform our world, just as his disciples transformed their world.

There's a story in this book, *Growing Places*. You may have heard about it. It will help you see what I mean. One night the author, Jay Kesler, was on a plane. It was beginning its descent into an airport in India. As the plane touched down, he noticed that both sides of the runway were lined with human bodies. He was shocked. Why were these people lying there on the concrete? Someone then told him that these were homeless people. This was where they slept. The runway soaked up heat during the day and kept them warm during the cold hours of the night.

Kesler took a bus to the city. As he walked from the bus station to his hotel, he saw further signs of poverty all about him. It was late, and the street was deserted. There was not a soul in sight.

Suddenly Kesler was startled by a strange sound: thump, scrape, thump, scrape, thump, scrape. He grew frightened. His heart began to pound. Then he turned around. There, just a few feet away, was a boy whose legs were cut off almost to the body. Under each arm was a tiny crutch. With a pathetic look on his face the boy held out his hands for some money. Jay gladly gave him all the coins he had. The pathetic look on the boy's face turned into a big smile.

There was a big lump in Jay's throat as he turned around and continued on toward the hotel. He hadn't gone ten feet when he heard a most God-awful sound. He turned around and saw a dozen other beggars swarming all over the boy. They were beating him with his own crutches, forcing him to give up his handful of coins. Kesler said he didn't sleep that night.

Into the midst of this poverty in India a woman came. She was on an errand from God. She looked about, almost in despair, at the deplorable conditions. She said to herself, "Something has to be done." She had only five rupees, the equivalent of two dollars, and the conviction that Jesus was calling her to work in this city.

With her five rupees she rented an old building. It had only a dirt floor, but it would have to do. Then she went around the neighborhood and volunteered to teach the small children. The old building became her school room. It had no desks, no chairs, no table. Her chalkboard was the dirt floor. She rubbed it smooth with an old rag and wrote on it with a wooden stick.

That was the way this woman began to attack the poverty and cruelty around her. It was a pathetic response. But what else could she do? It was either this or nothing. That woman refused to give in to despair. She took each day as it came and gave all she had to the work Jesus had given her.

Today, years later, what are the results? She has 80 fully equipped schools, 300 modern, mobile dispensaries, 70 leprosy clinics, 30 homes for the dying, 30 homes for abandoned children, and over 40,000 volunteers, worldwide, helping her.

What Jesus Is Asking of Us

Mother Teresa heard the voice of Jesus in the slums of Calcutta. She dared to take seriously his invitation to reach out to the least of his brothers and sisters. Mother Teresa's faith and courage are a living example of what Jesus is inviting us to do.

He is inviting us to continue his miracles today, by reaching out in love to those in need. He is saying to us: "I have no feet but your feet to carry me into the slums, the factories, and the offices of your cities. I have no hands but your hands to reach out to the helpless, the homeless, and the hopeless. I have no tongue but your tongue to tell my brothers and sisters why I came to live with them, and why I suffered and died for them. I have no help but your help to announce my Kingdom to the hungry and to invite them to the banquet prepared for them since the creation of the world."

MEDITATION/DISCUSSION POINTS

1. Describe a time when you prayed over a sick or troubled person, as Marta-Korwin Rhodes did. Recall a time when someone prayed over you. What effect did it have on you?

2. The book says, "The boy grew violent. He spoke ancient languages. And once, while helplessly strapped in bed, long red scratches appeared on his body." What convinces you most that some extraordinary evil power is at work in our world?

3. The author says, "It is impossible to force another to believe. Not even Jesus could do it, or wanted to do it." Describe a time when your faith seemed to go behind a cloud for a while. When and how did it return?

4. Jesus told his followers, "You are like salt for all mankind. . . . You are like light for the whole world." What is Jesus' point? What keeps you from being more of a light than you are?

5. The chapter ends, "I have no feet but yours . . . no hands but yours . . . no tongue but yours." Recall a time when someone was Jesus' feet, hands, or tongue for you.

"Listen, then, and learn what the parable of the sower means. . . . The seeds that fell among thorn bushes stand for those who hear the message; but the worries about this life and the love for riches choke the message, and they don't bear fruit." *Matthew 13:18, 22*

9. PARABLES OF JESUS

A man in ancient Baghdad sent his servant to the marketplace to buy some provisions. Shortly afterward the servant returned. He was pale and trembling from head to foot.

"Master," said the servant, "just a few minutes ago in the market, I was jostled rudely by a man in the crowd. When I turned to see who would do such a thing, I saw it was death. He looked at me in a very threatening way. Please lend me your fastest horse that I may flee to Samarra. Death will never think of looking for me there." The merchant gladly lent his servant his fastest horse. The servant mounted and galloped away in a burst of speed.

Meanwhile, the merchant went down to the marketplace to buy the provisions that the servant had failed to purchase. When he got there, lo and behold, who should be there but death. "Why did you look at my servant in such a threatening way this morning?" the merchant asked. "That wasn't a threatening look," said death. "It was a look of surprise. I was amazed to see him in Baghdad, for I had an appointment with him tonight in far-off Samarra."

That story by Somerset Maugham is one of my favorites. Storytelling has been popular ever since human beings learned to put words together to form sentences. As you know, ancient peoples couldn't read or write. Whenever they wanted to teach something important, they made up a story about it. This made the truth fun to learn and easy to remember.

The point of the story I just told was to help people come to grips with the mystery of death.

When your time to die comes, that's it. There's nothing you can do about it. There's no place you can go to hide from it.

Jesus the Storyteller

Jesus probably told more stories than most teachers. One reason Jesus told so many stories was because he wanted to teach people about his Father's Kingdom. And his Father's Kingdom was unlike anything anyone has ever seen or heard. It was something completely beyond our experience, even our imagination. Not even our wildest dream can compare to it.

Let me tell you another story to illustrate the problem Jesus faced when he tried to tell people about his Father's Kingdom. A teenager was looking through a magazine and listening to some records. A friend of the family who was deaf entered the room.

For a while he watched her tap her toe to the music. Then he asked her, "What does music sound like?" The girl thought for a moment. Then she smiled and stood in front of him. That way he could read her lips. As she talked, she made gestures with her hands, her face, and her body.

The friend watched her carefully and studied everything she did. But the more she spoke, and the more she gestured, the more confused he became. Finally the girl laughed. She shook her head and gave up. She realized that trying to describe sound to a deaf person was like trying to describe color to a blind person.

This story, from the movie *The Heart Is a Lonely Hunter*, gives us a small idea of the problem Jesus faced in telling people about his

Father's Kingdom. The notion of the Kingdom of God was way beyond people's ordinary human experience. Trying to describe it to them was like trying to describe music to a deaf person or color to a blind person.

Let me tell just one more story to make my point. This story concerns a fish who wandered off one day away from his underwater ocean village. As he swam along outside the village, he stopped suddenly. There, about a hundred feet ahead of him, was a monstrous machine. As he watched, several divers with camera equipment came out of the hatch door.

As the divers emerged, one by one, the fish studied their strange bodies. Each wore a terrifying face mask. Each carried frightening equipment. The poor fish began to panic. He had never seen anything like this. Turning around, he swam full speed back to his village. He told everyone he saw about the strange invaders from outer water.

Well, you can imagine his consternation when no one took him seriously. They laughed at him. "There can't be life in outer water!" they said. "Too much oxygen! Not enough water! What you saw were probably refractions from our own system."

Bridges to the Unknown

Maybe now you can get some idea of the hard time Jesus had in trying to tell people about God and God's Kingdom. Take, for example, the notion of God's loving concern for sinners. This idea just didn't make sense to most people. How could God, who was holy, love sinners, who were evil? How could God, who created the

137

stars, the sun, the moon, the rivers, and the mountains, be interested in ignorant misfits?

To help people grow in their understanding of God, Jesus told stories—special stories, called parables. Someone described a parable as "an earthly story with a heavenly meaning." And that's exactly what a parable is. It is a story about something we know that teaches us about something we don't know. To help us understand God's loving concern for every human being, even sinners and misfits, Jesus told this simple story.

"Suppose one of you has a hundred sheep and loses one of them—what does he do? He leaves the other ninety-nine sheep in the pasture and goes looking for the one that got lost until he finds it. When he finds it, he is so happy that he puts it on his shoulders and carries it back home. Then he calls his friends and neighbors together and says to them, 'I'm so happy I found my lost sheep. Let us celebrate!' In the same way, I tell you, there will be more joy in heaven over one sinner who repents than over ninety-nine respectable people who do not need to repent." (Luke 15:4-7)

The message contained in this story is really a hard one for some people to grasp. It is that God loves us unconditionally. That means that no matter how bad we are, God still loves us and wants us. And when we have strayed from him, he actively seeks us out, just as a shepherd seeks out a lost sheep.

Two Levels

The parables of Jesus, therefore, have two levels of understanding. First, there is the story itself: what Jesus said. Second, there is the meaning behind the story: what Jesus meant.

I once asked my students to write their own version of the parable of the lost sheep. In other words, I wanted them to think about how Jesus might tell that same story today, using a more up-to-date example. One student did it this way: "Suppose you just finished typing your term paper, and you discovered one sheet missing. What would you do? You would forget about the other ninety-nine sheets and go looking for the one lost sheet. When you find it, you are so happy that you take the other ninety-nine sheets, throw them into the air and say, 'Yippee! I found my lost sheet.' That's how God feels when you start back to church again."

Window Stories

Parables that teach us about God or God's Kingdom are sometimes called "window" parables. In other words, they are stories that serve as windows through which we can look to see what God or God's Kingdom is like.

In the parable of the lost sheep, God is like a concerned shepherd who goes out in search of the sheep that has strayed. When he finds it, he doesn't tie it to a tree and punish it. He carries it home, lovingly, on his shoulders. Let me give you another example of a window parable, a story that gives a picture of what God or God's Kingdom is like.

Not long ago, workmen in the Philippine Islands were digging at an irrigation project. Accidentally they came upon a buried treasure. It was a chest of solid gold objects, worth three million dollars. The gold was believed to be part of a treasure buried by the Japanese General Yamashita during World War II. The general was captured and hanged toward the end of the war, carrying to his grave the secret location of the buried treasure. When news of the discovery leaked out, thousands of people came with picks and shovels to dig in other parts of the field. "It's bedlam out there," said one policeman. "Work on the irrigation project is suspended because of the huge mob digging everywhere."

The news story reminded me of Jesus' parable of the buried treasure and his parable of the priceless pearl. Jesus told both these parables to give people an idea of what God's Kingdom is like. Jesus said:

> *"The Kingdom of heaven is like this. A man happens to find a treasure hidden in a field. He covers it up again, and is so happy that he goes and sells everything he has, and then goes back and buys that field.*
>
> *"Also, the Kingdom of heaven is like this. A man is looking for fine pearls, and when he finds one that is unusually fine, he goes and sells everything he has and buys that pearl."*
>
> *(Matthew 13:44-46)*

Both of these parables make the same point. The Kingdom of God is the answer to our dreams. It is everything we ever hoped for. It is everything we ever dreamed of. It is the answer to all our prayers. Nothing can compare to it. By putting the Kingdom of God above all else, we do not lose anything; we gain everything. God's Kingdom is joy without bounds. It is happiness beyond belief.

Mirror Stories

A window parable is a story that Jesus told to give us a picture of what God or God's Kingdom is like. Jesus also used "mirror" parables. Now what's a mirror parable? It is a story that serves as a mirror. You can look into the story and you get a true picture of yourself.

Let me explain what I mean. There's an unforgettable scene in *Hamlet*, where the young prince confronts his mother, the Queen. Hamlet is sure she played a part in the murder of his father, the King. Hamlet says, "Come, come and sit down. You shall not budge, you shall not go till I set up a glass where you may see the inmost part of you." His mother replies, "O Hamlet, speak no more. Thou turn mine eyes into my very soul. And there I see such black and grained spots."

The mirror that Hamlet set before his mother was not a glass mirror, but a word mirror. It forced her to see herself as she really was. Some of the parables of Jesus are like that. They are word mirrors. That is, they are stories into which we can look and see ourselves as we really are. In other words, they reflect back to us a true picture of our real selves. Here's an example. Jesus said:

"Once there was a man who went out to sow grain. As he scattered the seed in the field, some of it fell along the path, where it was stepped on, and the birds ate it up. Some of it fell on rocky ground, and when the plants sprouted, they dried up because the soil had no moisture. Some of the seed fell among thorn bushes, which grew up with the plants and choked them. And some seeds fell in good soil; the plants grew and bore grain, one hundred grains each."

His disciples asked Jesus what this parable meant, and he answered, ". . . The seeds that fell along the path stand for those who hear; but the Devil comes and takes the message away from their hearts in order to keep them from believing and being saved. The seeds that fell on rocky ground stand for those who hear the message and receive it gladly. But it does not sink deep into them; they believe only for a while but when the time of testing comes, they fall away. The seeds that fell among thorn bushes stand for those who hear; but the worries and riches and pleasures of this life crowd in and choke them, and their fruit never ripens. The seeds that fell in good soil stand for those who hear the message and retain it in a good and obedient heart, and they persist until they bear fruit."

(Luke 8:5-15)

The sower in the parable is Jesus. The seed is the word of Jesus. The four types of ground—path, rocky dirt, thorns, and good soil—are the four types of people who listened to Jesus.

First, there were the people whose hearts were hard, like the path. They were closed to the words of Jesus. They came to listen to him merely out of curiosity or to try to trip him up. Their hearts were not open.

Second, there were the people whose hearts were like the thin layer of soil on the top of the rocky ground. These people listened to what Jesus had to say. His message made sense to them. They received it gladly. But when the heat of temptation came, it dried up the words of Jesus, just as the sun dried up the sprouting seeds that fell into the shallow soil.

Third, there were the people whose hearts were like the patch of thorns. These people listened to what Jesus had to say. They, too, came to hear him because they were interested. They, too, responded joyfully. But when they got home, they got so involved in the affairs of life that they forgot everything Jesus said. The routine concerns of living choked the words of Jesus, killing them.

Finally, there were the people whose hearts were like the good soil. They were open to the message of Jesus. These people received his words eagerly. They took his message seriously. The seed that was sown in their hearts bore much fruit.

The message of the parable of the sower is this: A seed will grow only if it falls into good soil. The same is true of the word of Jesus. It will grow only if it falls into a good heart.

Invitations to Us

So Jesus is putting a mirror in front of us. He is asking us to look into it and to decide which of the four kinds of soil is our own heart most like. He says to us, "Is your heart like the path, hard and closed to my word? Or is your heart like the shallow layer of soil on the rock? Does it dry up when the heat of temptation comes, killing my word within you? Or is your heart like the patch of thorns? Do problems and pleasures of life crowd out and choke my word within you before it can grow and develop? Or is your heart like the good soil, completely open to my word, nourishing it and bearing much fruit?"

Now let me express the parable of the sower in a contemporary way, just as the student expressed the parable of the lost sheep in an updated or modern way.

Four businessmen are dressing after a fast, hard game of racquet ball. Their conversation turns to a retreat they had made on the previous weekend. Allen thought the weekend was a waste of time. He said most of the ideas presented on the retreat were too unrealistic.

Bill was more positive. He thought that most of the ideas presented made good sense. He was taken, especially, by the idea of setting aside a few minutes each day for personal prayer.

Charlie gave the retreat high marks also. He especially liked the idea of doing something to help the underprivileged. As a result, he had volunteered his Saturdays to work with juvenile delinquents.

Don was really excited. He bought the retreat one hundred percent. He, too, liked the idea of regular daily prayer. He also liked the idea that he and his wife should spend more time doing things together with their children.

Two months later the same four businessmen met together for lunch. The topic of the retreat came up again. Allen had not changed his mind about it. He didn't want to discuss it.

Bill was still very positive about the retreat. He admitted, however, that he had stopped his daily prayer program. It just didn't work out.

Charlie was also still very positive about the retreat. But when football season began, he discontinued his Saturday volunteer work. "I guess

I'm just an incurable TV football junkie," he laughed.

Don was as enthusiastic as ever. His wife was now praying with him, and his family was developing a real closeness through projects they were doing together.

And so Allen's experience corresponded to the seed that fell on the path. Bill's experience corresponded to the seed that fell on the rock. Charlie's experience corresponded to the seed that fell among thorns. And Don's experience corresponded to the seed that fell into good soil.

They Leave Us Free

Mirror parables, like the parable of the sower, help us to see ourselves in a new light. They do not point a finger right at us and accuse us. They merely show us a picture of ourselves and let us draw our own conclusion. In other words, they don't hit us over the head and say, "You're guilty!" They give us information about ourselves and let us decide. We are free either to accept what we see and do something about it, or to reject what we see and do nothing about it.

Another good example of a mirror parable is a story of David in the Second Book of Samuel in the Old Testament. David was a great leader in Israel. But like all of us, David was capable of great sinfulness. Once he went so far as to seduce the wife of one of his common soldiers.

Nathan, a prophet and advisor to David, felt compelled to confront the king about the terrible deed. But Nathan wanted to do it in a way that would make David himself see and admit how terrible his crime was.

Nathan decided to tell David a mirror parable. One day he went to David and said to him:

> "There were two men who lived in the same town; one was rich and the other poor. The rich man had many cattle and sheep, while the poor man had only one lamb . . . He took care of it, and it grew up in his home with his children. He would feed it some of his own food . . . One day a visitor arrived at the rich man's home. The rich man didn't want to kill one of his own animals to fix a meal for him; instead, he took the poor man's lamb and prepared a meal for his guest."

> David became very angry at the rich man and said, "I swear by the living LORD that the man who did this ought to die! . . ."

> "You are that man," Nathan said to David. "And this is what the LORD God of Israel says: '. . . Why, then, have you disobeyed my commands? Why did you do this evil thing? . . .' "

> [David hung his head and said,] "I have sinned against the LORD."

> (2 Samuel 12:1-9, 13)

Nathan's parable acted as a mirror in which David could see himself and his deed as they truly were. David's honesty in admitting his guilt and wanting to do something about it is a model for us. It shows us how we should respond to the mirror parables of Jesus.

The parables of Jesus, then, have two levels of understanding. First, there's the story level: what Jesus said. Second, there's the lesson level: what Jesus meant to teach through the story.

The parables of Jesus also fall into two main groups. First, there's the window parable. It's a symbol, drawn from daily life, that gives us a picture of what God's Kingdom is like. Second, there's the mirror parable. It's a story that helps us to see ourselves as we really are. Jesus' parable of the sower is such a story. Jesus holds up this mirror before each of us and asks us frankly: "Which seed bed is your own heart most like? How open are you to my word right now?"

Right Now!

I say "right now" because God is continually speaking his word to us. This is especially true if, like the lost sheep, we have strayed from him for whatever reason. God is not someone who abandons the sinner. He is a loving father who goes out in search of the sinner and brings him back lovingly on his shoulders.

Here's a final story to illustrate God's concern for those who stray from him by sin. It concerns a man I will call Bill. Bill was once a prominent contractor. But the pressure of his personal and business life caused him to turn to alcohol. In time, his wife and children left him and his business went bankrupt.

One day Bill was walking down the street. He happened to look down. There on the sidewalk was an old, bent, rusty nail. Bill thought to himself, "That nail is a perfect picture of myself. I, too, am rusty and bent out of shape. I am good for nothing but to be thrown away, as that nail was."

Bill bent down, picked up the nail, and put it in his pocket. When he got back home, he took a hammer and began pounding the nail straight. Then he took some sandpaper and sanded the rust off it. Bill then placed the nail next to a new one. You could hardly tell the difference between the two. A thought flashed through Bill's mind. His life could be straightened out and sanded clean again. But it would not be easy! Could he take the hard blows and the sanding? He decided to give it a try.

Today, Bill is reunited with his family and he is back in the construction business again. He owes everything to that old, rusty, bent nail that he found on the sidewalk at just the right time. To this day Bill keeps the restored nail in his wallet.

Let me conclude by paraphrasing the words of a song I heard years ago. They went something like this:

> Jesus was the storytellin' kind.
> He painted pictures in the mind.
> It was the way he showed people how
>   things were supposed to be.
> He used the sky. He used the sea.
> He used the birds. He used the tree.
> He used whatever he could see.
> Storyteller?
> Yes, Jesus was the storytellin' kind.
> He painted pictures in the mind.
> It was the way he helped us see
> what we—you and I—could really be.

MEDITATION/DISCUSSION POINTS

1. The book says, "Storytelling has been popular ever since human beings learned to put words together to form sentences." Recall a story (told to you by a parent, teacher, or in a sermon) that made a special impression on you.

2. The author says, "Jesus probably told more stories than most teachers." Of the stories Jesus told, which is one of your favorites and why?

3. The parable of the lost treasure indicates that the Kingdom of God "is everything we ever hoped for. It is everything we ever dreamed of." Recall one of the happiest, most fulfilling moments of your life.

4. Explain the difference between the seed that falls on rocky soil and the seed that falls among thorns. How do you try to combat the destructive influence of routine and the routine affairs in your life?

5. The book says, "To this day Bill keeps the restored nail in his wallet." Do you keep any special memento in your wallet? Recall and relive the story behind it.

The cup we use in the Lord's Supper and for which we give thanks to God: when we drink from it, we are sharing in the blood of Christ. And the bread we break: when we eat it, we are sharing in the body of Christ. *1 Corinthians 10:16*

10. LAST SUPPER OF JESUS

Some years ago I was studying in Europe. Since my background was architecture, I enjoyed visiting the new churches that had been built to replace those that had been destroyed during World War II.

One day I was really struck by a tabernacle door in a church in Cologne, Germany. It was divided into four panels. The first panel contained six shapes. After puzzling over the shapes for a few minutes, I concluded they stood for the six stone water jars described in the second chapter of the Gospel according to John:

There was a wedding in the town of Cana in Galilee . . . When the wine had given out . . . Jesus' mother then told the servants, "Do whatever [Jesus] tells you."

The Jews have rules about ritual washing, and for this purpose six stone water jars were there . . . Jesus said to the servants, "Fill these jars with water." They filled them to the brim, and then he told them, "Now draw some water out and take it to the man in charge of the feast." They took him the water, which now had turned into wine, and he tasted it . . . He called the bridegroom and said to him, "Everyone else serves the best wine first, and after the guests have drunk a lot, he serves the ordinary wine. But you have kept the best wine until now!"

(John 2:1-10)

The artist intended the first panel to refer to the first miracle of Jesus. He saved a young wedding couple from embarrassment by changing water into wine.

The second panel of the door contained seven shapes. This panel was easier to figure out. It referred to the five loaves and the two fishes that Jesus multiplied one day to feed a crowd of hungry people.

Jesus ... saw that a large crowd was coming to him, so he asked Philip, "Where can we buy enough food to feed all these people?" . . . Andrew, who was Simon Peter's brother, said, "There is a boy here who has five loaves of barley bread and two fish. But they will certainly not be enough for all these people."

"Make the people sit down," Jesus told them ... So all the people sat down; there were about five thousand men. Jesus took the bread, gave thanks to God, and distributed it to the people who were sitting there. He did the same with the fish, and they all had as much as they wanted. . . .

Seeing the miracle that Jesus had performed, the people there said, "Surely this is the prophet who was to come into the world!" Jesus knew that they were about to come and seize him in order to make him king by force; so he went off again to the hills by himself.

(John 6:5, 8-11, 14)

The next day the people went looking for Jesus. He told them:

"You are looking for me because you ate the bread . . . not because you understood my miracles. Do not work for food that spoils; instead, work for food that lasts for eternal life. This is the food which the Son of Man will give you. . . .

"The bread that I will give . . . is my flesh . . ." This started an angry argument among them.

"How can this man give us his flesh to eat?" they asked.

(John 6:26-27, 51-52)

So the second panel represented the miracle of the loaves and fishes. It was on the occasion of this miracle that Jesus promised to give us his own body to eat and his own blood to drink.

The third panel contained thirteen people, the middle figure slightly larger than the rest. They were seated at a table. It was obvious that these figures represented Jesus and the twelve apostles sharing the Last Supper together.

Jesus took a piece of bread, gave a prayer of thanks, broke it, and gave it to his disciples. "Take it," he said, "this is my body."

Then he took a cup, gave thanks to God, and handed it to them; and they all drank from it. Jesus said, "This is my blood which is poured out for many, my blood which seals God's covenant."

(Mark 14:22-24)

The fourth panel contained three people, the middle one slightly larger than the other two. All three were seated at a table. This panel was a little more difficult to figure out. Can you guess what the fourth panel referred to?

I concluded that it represented the supper Jesus ate at Emmaus with the disciples after his resurrection. It happened like this: Shortly after Jesus was crucified, two of his disciples were returning to their home in Emmaus. They were deeply troubled and saddened by the events of Good Friday. Suddenly a stranger came up behind them and asked if he could walk along with them. "Why are you so sad?" the stranger asked.

The two disciples told him the story of Jesus and how, since it was all over now, they were going back home. Thereupon the stranger, whom the two didn't recognize, said:

"Was it not necessary for the Messiah to suffer these things and then enter his glory?" And Jesus explained to them what was said about himself in all the scriptures, beginning with the books of Moses and the writing of all the prophets.

As they came near the village . . . Jesus acted as if he were going farther; but [the two disciples said,] "Stay with us; the day is almost over and it is getting dark." So he went in to stay with them. He sat down to eat with them, took the bread, and said the blessing; then he broke the bread and gave it to them. Then their eyes were opened and they recognized him.

So the artist intended the fourth panel to refer to the supper at Emmaus. At that time the risen Jesus revealed himself to two of his disciples in the breaking of the bread.

Why These Events?

Why do you suppose the artist picked these four events for the tabernacle door? I think that he wanted to tell us that he saw an important connection between the marriage feast of Cana, the multiplication of the loaves and fishes, the Last Supper, and the Emmaus supper.

What is the relationship between these four events? Let's begin with the marriage feast of Cana, where Jesus changed water into wine. Today some Christians have difficulty understanding this miracle. But early Christians had no problem with it at all. They were people close to the

154

soil. They simply said, "Why shouldn't the creator change water into wine? After all, God's own creation does it every day. The lowly grapevine sucks water out of the soil and, with help from the sun and a few bacteria, turns it into wine."

Prepares for Supper

But the important thing about the miracle of Cana is not how Jesus did it, but why he did it. Was it merely to save a young couple from embarrassment? The artist who designed the door thinks it was more than this. He suggests that Jesus had a deeper reason for performing the miracle. Jesus was preparing his disciples for an even greater miracle that he would perform at the Last Supper. Then, he would go a step further. He would change wine into his own blood.

We can describe the relationship of Cana to the Last Supper with the word *prepares*. The miracle of Cana set the stage, or prepared the disciples, for what Jesus would do at the Last Supper.

What about the second panel, the multiplication of the loaves and fishes? Again, some Christians today have difficulty with the performance of this miracle. But, again, early Christians had no problem with it. They simply said, "Well, what's so remarkable about feeding five thousand people with five loaves? Every year nature performs a similar miracle by turning five bushels of wheat into five hundred bushels."

The important thing again, however, is not how Jesus multiplied the five loaves, but why he multiplied them. Was it merely out of compassion for a hungry crowd? Again, the artist suggests that Jesus had a further reason for multiplying the loaves. This large crowd of over five thousand people provided an ideal setting for Jesus to make a remarkable promise. He promised the people that one day he would feed them more marvelously than he had just done. He would even feed them more marvelously than Moses had fed their ancestors. Jesus said to the people:

"What Moses gave you was not the bread from heaven. . . . I am the living bread that came down from heaven. If anyone eats this bread, he will live forever. The bread that I will give him is my flesh. . . ."

(John 6:32, 51)

Promises Supper

The fulfillment of this promise came at the Last Supper. The miracle of the loaves was a promise of what was to happen at the Last Supper. Jesus used the occasion to promise that he would give his own body to eat and his own blood to drink.

So we may describe the connection between the miracle of the loaves and fishes and the Last Supper with the word *promises.* Sometimes Christians attach yet another meaning to the multiplication of the loaves and fishes. It has to do with the boy's personal gift of five loaves and two fishes.

Pope John Paul II referred to this meaning in a meeting with young people during his visit to Scotland. He reminded the young people that the apostle Andrew, the patron saint of Scotland, was the same apostle who told Jesus about the boy who had five loaves and two fishes. Then he said, "Andrew gave Jesus all that was available, and Jesus miraculously fed those five thousand people and still had something left over. It is exactly the same with our lives. Left alone to face the difficult challenges of life today, you feel conscious of your own inadequacy and afraid of what the future may hold for you. But what I say to you is this: place yourselves in the hands of Jesus. He will accept you and bless you, and he will make such use of your lives as will be beyond our greatest expectations."

In other words, the miracle of the loaves and fishes is an invitation to all Christians to place their talents at the service of Jesus. At first, one's individual talents may seem trivial, almost as trivial as five loaves and two fishes. But when placed in the hands of Jesus, these talents can become important. In other words, Jesus can multiply them beyond our wildest dreams.

The Supper

This brings us to the third panel on the door, that is, the Last Supper. Before discussing the Last Supper, let me give you some background. There's a novel by Elie Wiesel called *The Town Beyond the Wall.* On one occasion in this book, a young man named Michael is able to live through torture because he draws strength from a close friend. The strength, however, does not come from the friend directly, but from Michael's memory of him. The story illustrates an important point about the biblical idea of remembering.

In the time of Jesus, the purpose behind Jewish religious celebrations was to remember what God had done for the Jewish people in times past. But when Jews remembered within the context of religious worship, they believed they did much more than merely call to mind some past event. They believed that in some unexplainable way they actually became a part of the event they were remembering. In other words, they participated in the event in some real way.

In this way, they shared in the event and received from it the same blessings that God gave to their ancestors through the event. For example, when Jews gathered to eat the Passover meal, they remembered how their ancestors passed over from slavery to freedom as God's chosen people. And in the process of remembering this event each year, they relived it in a spiritual way.

It was with this in mind that Jesus and his apostles gathered together to eat the Passover meal on the night before Jesus died. Jews ate the Passover meal just after the first stars appeared. This enabled them to eat the meal at the same time as one family.

When the first stars appeared, Jesus acted as the father of the family and began the Passover ceremonies. He began by washing the feet of the apostles. This surprised the apostles. Although feet washing was customary at some ancient banquets, it was not done at Passover meals.

In ancient times, washing another's feet was a servant's job. No free citizen could be forced to do it. So this action of Jesus created a deep impression on his disciples. When Jesus finished, he said:

"I, your Lord and Teacher, have just washed your feet. You, then, should wash one another's feet. I have set an example for you, so that you will do just what I have done . . . How happy you will be if you put it into practice!"

(John 13:14-15, 17)

158

Jesus then took a cup of wine. He passed it around to the others. The apostles knew the meaning of drinking from the same cup. It was a sign of their solidarity not only with those sitting around the table but with Jews everywhere celebrating the Passover meal.

Ordinarily the first food that was eaten at Jewish meals was bread. The Passover meal, however, began with the eating of bitter herbs. This provided the occasion for the youngest person present to ask, "Why is tonight's meal different?" The father of the family would then explain the meaning of the foods eaten at the Passover meal.

The bitter herbs "remembered" the years of bitter slavery in Egypt. The lamb "remembered" the Lord's command to slaughter a lamb for sacrifice and to smear its blood on the door of the house to save it from the tenth plague in Egypt. The unleavened bread "remembered" the haste with which their ancestors fled from Egypt after the tenth plague. They did not even wait for the next day's bread to rise.

This Is My Body

After the eating of the herbs and the explanation of the foods, the meal itself began. It was at this point that:

> [Jesus] took a piece of bread, gave thanks to God, broke it, and gave it to [his disciples], saying, "This is my body, which is given for you. Do this in memory of me."
>
> (Luke 22:19)

These words of Jesus were surprising and totally unexpected. Some of the apostles must have recalled the words spoken by Jesus months earlier, on a sunny hillside in Galilee:

"I am the living bread that came down from heaven. If anyone eats this bread, he will live forever. The bread that I will give him is my flesh."
(John 6:51)

One by one, the apostles ate the bread which Jesus had blessed. It was a solemn moment. The apostles would remember it the rest of their lives. When all had shared the bread, Jesus passed the Passover lamb. As he did, these words of the prophet Isaiah probably came to mind: "Like a lamb about to be slaughtered . . . he was put to death for the sins of our people. . . . He took the place of many sinners and prayed that they might be forgiven."

This Is My Blood

When everyone had eaten, it was time to drink the cup of wine. This, too, was part of the special ritual of the Passover meal. At this point,

[Jesus] took the cup and said, "This cup is God's new covenant, sealed with my blood. Whenever you drink it, do so in memory of me."
(1 Corinthians 11:25)

Once again, the apostles were struck by the words of Jesus. They brought to mind God's first covenant with his chosen people. On that occasion, Moses sprinkled blood on the people, saying, "This is the blood that seals the covenant which the LORD made with you." Perhaps some of the apostles recalled, also, the words of Jeremiah: "The time is coming when I will make a new covenant with the people of Israel and with the people of Judah."

One by one, the apostles drank from the cup. Again, it was a solemn moment. When everyone had shared the cup, Jesus led them in singing the song that concluded the Passover meal.

Do This in Memory of Me

After the meal, Jesus invited the apostles to go with him to the Mount of Olives, just outside the city walls of Jerusalem. The disciples were happy as they walked along under the stars. But their happiness was not without some shadow. Jesus had said too many disturbing things during the meal. His final words, especially "Do this in memory of me," made them wonder.

Years later, Paul referred to this command of Jesus when he said,

Every time you eat this bread and drink from this cup you proclaim the Lord's death until he comes.

(1 Corinthians 11:26)

Paul's words are important for us. Jesus is truly present today every time we celebrate the Lord's Supper. But the fullness of his presence among us will not be realized until he comes again. We bear witness to this when we proclaim together in our celebrations of the Lord's Supper: "Christ has died, Christ is risen, Christ will come again." This is the most important proclamation the Christian community makes to the modern world.

And so the artist dedicated the third panel of the door to the Last Supper, when Jesus established the new covenant.

Celebrates Supper

In the fourth panel, the artist portrays what may have been the first celebration of the Lord's Supper. Certainly Luke's description of the Emmaus supper seems to support the artist's interpretation. It matches his description of the Last Supper. Luke writes:

> [Jesus] . . . took the bread, and said the blessing; then he broke the bread and gave it to them. Then their eyes were opened and they recognized him, but he disappeared from their sight.
>
> (Luke 24:30-31)

And so we may describe the relationship of the Emmaus supper to the Last Supper with the word *celebrates*. When the two disciples left Jerusalem to return to Emmaus, they were in total despair. Their dream that Jesus had come to establish God's Kingdom on earth had turned into a nightmare on Good Friday afternoon. And now with the same suddenness, that situation of despair was reversed. They had just met Jesus, risen and alive. What they never thought could happen did happen. Jesus had triumphed over death.

The artist's door with its four panels makes a remarkable summary of the biblical story of the Last Supper. It traces it from Cana, where it was prepared, to Capernaum, where it was promised, to Jerusalem, where it was established, to Emmaus, where it was celebrated.

Striking Similarity

Whenever I meditate on the Emmaus supper, I am struck by the similarity between the situation of the Emmaus disciples and the situation of many people today. As children we first hear the story of Jesus from our parents. It is an exciting story of a Jesus who loves us very much. But then, as we pass out of childhood, Jesus often passes out of our lives also. Like the two disciples, we leave behind the Jesus of our childhood in some unmarked tomb. We go on our way alone. All we have left of Jesus are memories. Jesus is no longer a person, only a childhood recollection.

And so, like the disciples of Emmaus, we go our own way, trying to come to grips with a world without Jesus. Then something totally unexpected happens. A stranger comes walking along. And a conversation follows. We tell the stranger about our broken dream. The stranger listens compassionately. Then he says something marvelous: "Was it not necessary for the Messiah to suffer these things?" That is, "Wasn't it necessary for the Jesus of your childhood to die, so that the Jesus of your adulthood could be born?"

And suddenly the stranger puts everything in a totally new light. We want to hear more. We invite the stranger to dinner. And while he breaks bread with us, we discover not a stranger, but Jesus. We discover a Jesus we had never known before. He is the risen Jesus. He is a more exciting Jesus than we ever imagined in our wildest dream.

No Other Jesus

I think of this whenever I hear a person say, "I believe in God, and I believe in Jesus, but I don't believe in the church." Whenever I hear this, I want to cry out, "But there is no Jesus apart from the church. The Jesus you are talking about no longer exists. He died on Calvary. The only Jesus there is today is the Jesus of Easter Sunday. He is the Jesus who has risen from the dead and lives on in the body of his followers. To try to separate Jesus from his followers, the community of believers, is like trying to separate your own head from your own body."

The Apostle Paul puts it this way: "Christ is like a single body." (1 Corinthians 12:12) "The church is Christ's body." (Ephesians 1:23) "Jesus is the head of his body, the church; he is the source of the body's life." (Colossians 1:18)

Allow me to conclude with a prayer. Lord Jesus, look kindly on those of us who have left you behind for dead in some unmarked grave. Come to us, as you did to the disciples walking back to Emmaus on Easter Sunday. Explain to us the scriptures again, as you did to those disciples. Stir up in us the fires of faith that still smoulder in our hearts. Sit down with us at table again, just as we did in times past. Let us experience you again in all your risen glory in the breaking of the bread.

MEDITATION/DISCUSSION POINTS

1. Pope John Paul II said, "Place yourself in the hands of Jesus. He will . . . make such use of your lives as will be beyond your greatest expectations." To what extent have you given your life to Jesus—placed your talents in his hands for his use?

2. Recall a time when Jesus used your talents (five loaves and two fish) to do something special for his cause.

3. In *The Town Beyond the Wall*, Michael is able to live through torture because he draws strength from the memory of a friend. Recall

the memory of a friend who is a source of strength to you.

4. Jesus said, "Do this in memory of me." Recall a celebration of the Lord's Supper that was especially meaningful to you. What is your main motivation for sharing in the Lord's Supper?

5. The book says that like the two Emmaus disciples, some people leave Jesus behind in some unmarked grave and go off for a while without him. Did you ever do this? What brought you back to Jesus?

My God, my God, why have you abandoned me? *Psalm 22:1*

11. SUFFERING OF JESUS

If you have ever been to the Holy Land, you know what an excellent view of Jerusalem you get from the Mount of Olives. On some days the view is absolutely breathtaking. It was on the Mount of Olives that Jesus began the suffering that led to his death. On the slopes of this mount still stand eight old olive trees. Nobody knows how old the trees are. One Roman historian says that ancient peoples believed that olive trees lived forever. Perhaps that's because old olive trees frequently generate new shoots. These new shoots then grow into young trees. Eventually the parent tree dies, leaving the young trees to carry on where the parent tree left off.

It may well be, therefore, that the eight old olive trees mark the exact spot where Jesus began the suffering that ended in his death. The gospel tells us that after the Last Supper, Jesus and his disciples left the supper room and headed for the Mount of Olives. The distance to the mount was probably a little over a mile. No doubt Jesus and his disciples walked much of the distance in prayerful silence.

Jesus' Prophecy

When the small group reached the foot of the Mount of Olives, they paused.

Then Jesus said to the disciples, "This very night all of you will run away and leave me, for the scripture says, 'God will strike the shepherd, and the sheep of the flock will be scattered.'"

(Matthew 26:31)

Well, as you might expect, these words broke the silence like a thunderclap. Peter's first reaction was to blurt out:

"I will never leave you, even though all the rest do." Jesus said to Peter, "I tell you that before the rooster crows tonight, you will say three times that you do not know me." Peter answered, "I will never say that, even if I have to die with you!" And all the other disciples said the same thing.
(Matthew 26:33-35)

Jesus didn't say any more, but he led the disciples to a small orchard on the mount, called the garden of Gethsemane. The word *Gethsemane* means "olive press." The name suggests that the place contained the equipment for extracting oil from olives. The apparatus was probably housed in a cave, perhaps one of those still visible on the mount.

Jesus' Prayer

The gospels indicate that Jesus visited Gethsemane frequently. It may be that the orchard belonged to a friend, possibly a well-to-do family like Mark's. Rich families owned orchards and farms outside the walls of the city. When they arrived at Gethsemane, Jesus said to the small group:

"Sit here while I go over there and pray." He took with him Peter and the two sons of Zebedee.
(Matthew 26:36-37)

At every important crossroad in his life, Jesus prayed. For example, he prayed at his baptism. He prayed before starting his preaching ministry. He prayed before choosing his twelve apostles.

He prayed before asking his apostles that all-important question, "Who do you say I am?" He prayed on that glorious day when he was transfigured on the mountain.

Ironically, the same three apostles who were with Jesus then were with him now. They had shared his hour of glory. Now they would share his hour of agony.

> Grief and anguish came over Jesus, and he said to Peter, James, and John, "The sorrow in my heart is so great that it almost crushes me. ..." He went a little farther on, threw himself face downward on the ground, and prayed, "My Father, if it is possible, take this cup of suffering from me! Yet not what I want, but what you want."
> (Matthew 26:37-39)

Jesus' Mental Suffering

In Gethsemane, Jesus begins a process of four sufferings that will lead to his death. His first suffering is mental agony. Jesus anticipates the physical suffering that he knew lay ahead of him. Such anticipation can be even more terrifying than physical suffering itself.

For months Jesus had been on a collision course with the authorities in Jerusalem. He had seen the tension between them and him mount month by month, week by week, day by day, and now, hour by hour.

Jesus had warned his disciples about the inevitable outcome of this mounting tension. He said to them:

> "The Son of Man will be handed over to the chief priests and the teachers of the Law. They will condemn him to death and then hand him

over to the Gentiles, who will make fun of him, whip him, and crucify him."

(Matthew 20:18-19)

But the warning went right over the heads of the disciples. Mark tells us that Peter actually rebuked Jesus for thinking such thoughts. And so Jesus suffered alone in his agony. He knew exactly what lay ahead for him in the next forty-eight hours.

Jesus had seen the Romans flog victims with whips. He had also seen them crucify victims. Crucifixion has been called the cruelist punishment ever devised. The words of the prophet Isaiah raced through his mind:

I bared my back to those who beat me. I did not stop them when they insulted me . . . and spit in my face. . . . Because of our sins he was wounded, beaten because of the evil we did. We are healed by the punishment he suffered, made whole by the blows he received. . . . Many people were shocked when they saw him; he was so disfigured that he hardly looked human.

(Isaiah 50:6; 53:5; 52:14)

As Jesus lay on the ground in agony, the words of the psalmist also came to mind:

Many enemies surround me . . . like fierce bulls. . . . My strength is gone, gone like water spilled on the ground. . . . My heart is like melted wax.

(Psalm 22:12-14)

In his agony, Jesus turned to his Father.

"If it is possible, take this cup of suffering from me! Yet not what I want, but what you want."

(Matthew 26:39)

A few years ago, I got a new insight into the agony of Jesus from a book by Martin Luther King. King was also on a collision course with authorities. He too had seen the tension between the authorities and himself mount month by month, week by week, and day by day.

Martin Luther King could see the handwriting on the wall. One night he got into bed. It had been a long day and he was tired. Just as he was about to doze off, the phone rang. King picked it up. A voice on the other end said: "Listen, nigger, we've taken all we want from you. Before next week, you'll be sorry you ever came to Montgomery."

Dr. King hung up. Suddenly, all his fears began to take hold of him. His courage began to leave him. He began to feel sick. He got up and started pacing the floor. He went to the kitchen, heated a pot of coffee, poured out a cup, and just sat there. He didn't know what to do or where to turn. Then he bowed his head and began to pray. The words he prayed that night went something like this: Lord, I am taking a stand for what I believe is right. But now I am afraid, deeply afraid. People are depending on me for leadership. If I am without strength or courage, they too will grow fearful. I am at the end of my rope. I don't know where to turn. I don't know what to do. I can no longer face this responsibility alone.

At that moment, said Dr. King later, "I experienced the presence of the divine as I have never experienced him before."

King's experience gives us an insight into how Jesus must have felt his Father's presence after his prayer in the garden. For when he finished praying, Luke says, "An angel from heaven appeared to Jesus and strengthened him."

Soon the sound of voices began to echo in the distance. They grew louder and louder, a sign that they were approaching. Jesus knew exactly what this meant.

In a few minutes a large number of soldiers entered the garden. Judas was with them:

> Judas went straight to Jesus and said, "Peace be with you, Teacher," and kissed him. Jesus answered, "Be quick about it, friend!" Then the soldiers came up, arrested Jesus, and held him tight. . . . Then all the disciples left him and ran away.
>
> (Matthew 26:49-50, 56)

Jesus' Emotional Suffering

Now a second suffering began for Jesus. In addition to his mental suffering, Jesus experienced a deep emotional suffering. It began when Judas betrayed him. It intensified when the rest of his disciples fled, leaving him to face his enemies alone.

The soldiers took Jesus to the house of Caiaphas, the High Priest. Peter had seen them leave the garden and was following them at a distance. When they arrived at the house of Caiaphas, Peter drew nearer to see what would happen. Suddenly someone spotted Peter and accused him of being a follower of Jesus. Peter denied the charge. Again someone pointed at Peter and accused him of being a disciple of Jesus. Again Peter denied the charge. And when he was accused for a third time, Peter shouted:

"I don't know what you are talking about!" At once, while he was still speaking, a rooster crowed. The Lord turned around and looked straight at Peter, and Peter remembered that the Lord had said to him, "Before the rooster crows tonight, you will say three times that you do not know me." Peter went out and wept bitterly.

(Luke 22:60-62)

The soldiers led Jesus to prison. They slammed the doors and bolted them. Jesus sat all alone in the dark. The mental agony of Jesus at Gethsemane was almost more than Jesus could bear. But now the emotional agony of having been betrayed, deserted, and denied nearly crushed the heart of Jesus. The words of Psalm 41 were now fulfilled: "Even my best friend . . . the one who shared my food, has turned against me."

We can only imagine the thoughts that went through the mind of Jesus as he lay, alone, on the stone floor of the prison dungeon. The next morning Jesus was led away. He was taken to be tried before the Jewish High Council.

"Tell us," they said, "are you the Messiah?" Jesus answered, "If I tell you, you will not believe me; and if I ask you a question, you will not answer. But from now on the Son of Man will be seated at the right side of Almighty God." They all said, "Are you, then, the Son of God?" He answered them, "You say that I am." And they said, "We don't need any witnesses! We ourselves have heard what he said!"

(Luke 22:67-71)

With that, Jesus was taken to the headquarters of the Roman governor, Pilate. The council hoped to get Pilate to pronounce the death sentence of Jesus. After questioning all parties concerned, Pilate sized up the situation as a religious struggle between Jews. So he tried to wash his hands of the situation.

Jesus' Physical Suffering

When every effort failed, Pilate gave up in utter frustration. He had Jesus flogged and handed him over for crucifixion. Jesus now began his third suffering. It was the suffering of physical pain.

The Jews were very familiar with flogging. They had practiced it themselves from ancient time, but only for serious offenses. The Book of Deuteronomy says:

The number of lashes will depend on the crime the offender has committed. He may be given as many as forty lashes, but no more; more than that would humiliate him publicly.

(Deuteronomy 25:2-3)

Romans were not so humane. They did not limit lashes, and they used whips designed to dig deeply into the victim's body. Roman writers tell us that victims sometimes collapsed and died before the beating was over.

It was to this kind of cruel punishment that Jesus was subjected. When the terrifying ordeal was over, the Roman soldiers mocked Jesus.

They made a crown out of thorny branches and placed it on his head, and put a stick in his right hand; then they knelt before him and made fun of him. "Long live the King of the Jews!" they said. They spat on him, and took the stick and hit him over the head. When they had finished making fun of him . . . they led him out to crucify him.

(Matthew 27:29-31)

174

I want to pause for a moment to tell you about Dr. Sheila Cassidy. I think her story has relevence here. In the 1970s Dr. Cassidy was serving as a medical doctor in Chile. One day a wounded man came to her for treatment. He was unable to go to a hospital because the secret police were after him.

Shortly afterward, Dr. Cassidy was arrested by the secret police. They took her to a prison, stripped her of her clothes, and stretched her out in a defenseless way. She writes, "I was subjected to a lot of physical pain and threatened with death. For the first time in my life I thought I was going to die. They were trying to force me to name people. . . . I was experiencing in some slight way what Christ had suffered. All during the hard, very hard time I just felt that he was there, and I asked him to help me hang on.

"After four days of physical pain, I was moved . . . I was left completely alone in a small room . . . I was filled with an enormous amount of fear that any moment they would come back and torture me again. I remembered the prayer Dietrich Bonhoeffer wrote while he was awaiting execution in a Nazi prison camp . . . "In me there is darkness, but with thee there is light. . . . Lord, whatsoever this day may bring, thy name be praised."

As Jesus was marched to the execution site, his physical suffering mounted and intensified severely. It was a custom in the ancient world to have the prisoner carry his own instrument of execution. Jesus was no exception. The cross on which he was to be nailed lay heavy on his shoulder, already raw from the flogging he had received.

After a few hundred yards Jesus began to grow weak from loss of blood. He became unsteady under the weight of his cross. So the soldiers forced a bystander, named Simon of Cyrene, to help him.

The distance from Pilate's headquarters to Golgotha, the execution site, was about a quarter of a mile. Golgotha was a small hill outside the city gate. The word itself means "Place of the Skull." The streets leading to Golgotha were narrow and paved with large stones. These stones were worn smooth and slippery from years of use.

On this day the streets were jammed with people. When the procession finally reached Golgotha, the hill was quickly ringed with helmeted Roman soldiers. Their job was to hold back the crowd.

Jesus was stripped and prepared for execution. At the last minute, the soldiers offered Jesus a drugged drink to deaden his mind to the ordeal. This was common practice. Jesus refused the drug.

After Jesus had been nailed to the cross, it was then lifted to an upright position. The horror of crucifixion consists of the pain involved in the process of dying. The pain is excruciating, but not enough to kill. The victim often ended up dying of hunger or thirst. One report says that criminals were known to have lingered for days, finally dying stark raving mad. It was this kind of suffering that Jesus suffered.

Jesus' Spiritual Suffering

As if this weren't enough, Jesus now began to endure a fourth suffering. It was spiritual suffering. Spiritual suffering is perhaps the most painful of all sufferings. It is the suffering of being abandoned in one's time of need. It is the suffering of being ridiculed in one's hour of torment.

People passing by shook their heads and hurled insults at Jesus: "Aha! You were going to tear down the Temple and build it back up in three days! Now come down from the cross and save yourself!"

(Mark 15:29-30)

Jesus heard their words. They cut deeply into his soul. Jesus responded by praying:

"Forgive them, Father! They don't know what they are doing." . . . At noon the whole country was covered with darkness, which lasted for three hours. At three o'clock Jesus cried out with a loud shout, "Eloi, Eloi, lema sabachthani?" which means, "My God, my God, why did you abandon me?"

(Luke 23:34; Mark 15:33-34)

A time comes in every life when we are helpless, when our friends can't help us, when we can't help ourselves. This time of spiritual suffering came for Jesus as he hung upon the cross. Even God seemed to abandon him. Jesus was alone in his torment. Again he turned to prayer:

My God, my God, why have you abandoned me? I have cried desperately for help, but still it does not come . . . I am no longer a man; I am a worm, despised and scorned by everyone! . . . My

177

strength is gone, gone like water spilled on the ground. All my bones are out of joint; my heart is like melted wax. My throat is as dry as dust, and my tongue sticks to the roof of my mouth. . . . All my bones can be seen. My enemies look at me and stare. They gamble for my clothes and divide them among themselves. O LORD, don't stay away from me! Come quickly to my rescue!

(Psalm 22:1, 6, 14-19)

But God did not come to rescue Jesus! Eventually the four sufferings of Jesus took their inevitable toll. Death came for Jesus.

It was about twelve o'clock when the sun stopped shining and darkness covered the whole country until three o'clock; and the curtain hanging in the Temple was torn in two. Jesus cried out in a loud voice, "Father! In your hands I place my spirit!" He said this and died.

(Luke 23:44-46)

When the Roman soldier at the foot of the cross saw everything that had happened, he cried out, "This man was really the Son of God!"

And so the crucifixion scene ends with all eyes fixed on the suffering man on the cross. Death has finally liberated Jesus from his suffering. And as he hangs there we ask ourselves: Why did Jesus, the Son of God, have to endure such incredible suffering: the mental suffering of anticipation in the garden; the emotional suffering of being betrayed, deserted, and denied by friends; the physical suffering of being flogged, crowned with thorns, and crucified; the spiritual suffering of feeling totally abandoned, even by God?

Why did Jesus die racked with every kind of human pain? Not because suffering is something valuable. Not because suffering is something good. Not at all!

Manifestation

It is not the suffering of Jesus that counts. It is the love of a Jesus who is willing to suffer that counts. The crucified body of Jesus framed against the sky speaks to us of love in three ways. First, it is a manifestation of love. The body of Jesus on the cross says in a visual way what Jesus had said so often in a verbal way: "The greatest love a person can have for his friends is to give up his life for them."

Revelation

Second, the body of Christ framed against the sky is a revelation about love. It tells us that love entails suffering. The body of Jesus on the cross says in a visual way what Jesus had said so often in a verbal way: "If anyone wants to come with me, he must forget himself, take up his cross every day and follow me."

And finally, the crucified body of Jesus framed against the sky is an invitation to love. It says: "Love one another just as I love you."

Invitation

And so the body of Jesus on the cross is a manifestation of love, a revelation about love, and an invitation to love.

Let me close with a prayer. Lord, teach me to be generous. Teach me to serve you as you deserve; to give and not to count the cost; to fight and not to heed the wounds; to toil and not to seek for rest; to labor and not to ask for reward, except to know that I am doing your will.

MEDITATION/DISCUSSION POINTS

1. "I am at the end of my rope. . . . I can no longer face this responsibility alone." At that moment, said Dr. King later, "I experienced the presence of the divine as I have never experienced him before." Recall a similar experience like this from your own life.

2. Dr. Sheila Cassidy said, "I was filled with an enormous amount of fear. . . . I remembered a prayer Dietrich Bonhoeffer wrote while he was waiting execution. . . . 'In me there is darkness, but with thee there is light. Lord, whatsoever this day may bring, thy name be praised.'" What prayer do you fall back on in times of trial? Why?

3. Jesus said, "Forgive them, Father! They don't know what they are doing." Recall a time when you prayed in a special way for your enemies.

4. "The body of Jesus on the cross is a manifestation of love, a revelation to love, and an invitation to love." Review each point. Which speaks to you in a special way?

5. Jesus experienced four sufferings: mental, emotional, physical and spiritual. Review each. Recall times when you endured these same sufferings.

For this reason God raised him to the highest place above and gave him the name that is greater than any other name. And so, in honor of the name of Jesus all beings in heaven, on earth, and in the world below will fall on their knees, and all will openly proclaim that Jesus Christ is Lord.... *Philippians 2:9–11*

12. RISING OF JESUS

It was a real hot afternoon. The famous Hollywood film director Cecil B. DeMille was drifting in a canoe on a lake in northern Maine. He was reading a book. He looked away from the book momentarily, down into the lake. There were a bunch of beetles in the water playing.

Suddenly one of the beetles began crawling up the side of the canoe. When it got halfway up, it attached the talons of its legs to the side of the canoe and died.

DeMille watched it for a minute; then he turned back to his book. About three hours later, DeMille looked down at the dead beetle again. What he saw amazed him. The beetle had dried up and its back was starting to crack open. As he watched, something began to emerge from the opening: first a moist head, and then wings. It was a beautiful dragonfly.

DeMille sat there in awe. Then the dragonfly began to move its wings. It hovered gracefully just a few inches above the water where the other beetles were still at play. Did they recognize the dragonfly? Did they realize that it was the same beetle that they had been playing with a few hours before?

DeMille took his finger and nudged the dried-up shell of the beetle. It was like an empty tomb. As it fell to the water below, several beetles came over to see what it was. When they saw it was a dead shell, they backed away from it.

Easter Experience

DeMille's experience may help us appreciate

better what happened in Jerusalem on Easter morning.

> Very early on Sunday morning the women went to the tomb [of Jesus], carrying the spices they had prepared. They found the stone rolled away from the entrance to the tomb, so they went in; but they did not find the body of the Lord Jesus. They stood there puzzled about this, when suddenly two men in bright shining clothes stood by them. Full of fear, the women bowed down to the ground as the men said to them, "Why are you looking among the dead for one who is alive? [Jesus] is not here; he has been raised."
>
> (Luke 24:1-6)

I'd like to stretch my water beetle analogy a little further. Jesus died nailed to a cross. The beetle died fastened to a canoe. Jesus underwent an amazing transformation three days after his death. The beetle underwent an amazing transformation three hours after its death. Jesus was not recognized by those who had been with him three days earlier. The beetle was not recognized by those who had been with it three hours earlier. The risen body of Jesus had new powers to move about. The beetle could now fly and no longer had to crawl about.

Risen Body

This is a beautiful example from nature that may help us understand better what happened to Jesus on Easter morning. The risen body of Jesus was totally different from the body of Jesus that was buried in the tomb. It was not a body that had miraculously returned to the same life it had before. It was a body that had made a quantum leap forward into a higher life.

In other words, the body of Jesus was not a revived body, like the body of Lazarus, the body of the son of the widow of Naim, or the body of the daughter of Jairus. The body of Jesus was a resurrected body. It was glorified. This means it was totally different from his previous body.

Paul compares the human body before resurrection to a seed, and the body after resurrection to the plant that emerges from the seed. He writes in 1 Corinthians:

Someone will ask, "How can the dead be raised to life? . . ." You fool! When you plant a seed in the ground, it does not sprout to life unless it dies. And what you plant is a bare seed, perhaps a grain of wheat or some other grain, not the full-bodied plant that will later grow up. God provides that seed with the body he wishes; he gives each seed its own proper body. . . .

This is how it will be when the dead are raised to life. When the body is buried, it is mortal; when raised, it will be immortal. When buried, it is ugly and weak; when raised, it will be beautiful and strong. When buried, it is a physical body; when raised, it will be a spiritual body.

(1 Corinthians 15:35-38, 42-44)

Because the body of Jesus is a glorified body, it was totally different from the body he had during his lifetime. This explains why the apostles had trouble recognizing Jesus at first after his resurrection.

For example, when Jesus appeared on the sea-shore of Galilee, John says, "Jesus stood at the water's edge, but the disciples did not know that it was Jesus." When Jesus appeared in the upper room to the apostles, Luke says, "They were terrified, thinking that they were seeing a ghost." And when Jesus appeared to Mary Magdelene, John says, "She turned around and saw Jesus standing there; but she did not know that it was Jesus."

Experiencing Jesus

All of this gives us some notion about the nature of the resurrected body. After the resurrection, the body of Jesus resided in a totally new dimension of reality. Jesus no longer walked among us as one of us. He walked among us as risen and glorified. And Jesus continues to be present among us today in the same way.

We cannot see Jesus as the people of Jericho saw him reach out his hand and heal the blind begger. We cannot hear Jesus as the people on the mountainside heard him explain the Kingdom of God. We cannot touch Jesus as the crowds reached out to touch his clothes and be cured as he walked through the streets of Capernaum.

But Jesus is present among us today, just as certainly as he was in Jericho, on the mountainside, or at Capernaum. The body of Jesus is no longer subject to the laws of space and time. The risen Jesus lives in a dimension of reality where space and time no longer exist.

What the psalmist says of God can now be said of Jesus because he is risen:

Where could I go to escape you? Where could I get away from your presence? If I went up to heaven, you would be there; if I lay down in the world of the dead, you would be there. If I flew away beyond the east or lived in the farthest place in the west, you would be there to lead me. . . . I could ask the darkness to hide me or the light around me to turn into night, but even darkness is not dark for you, and the night is as bright as the day. Darkness and light are the same to you.

(Psalm 139:7-12)

If Jesus exists in a dimension of reality that our senses cannot penetrate, what is the difference between that and not being present to us at all? How can a glorified Jesus influence our lives? How can a glorified Jesus touch our hearts? How is it possible for us to experience the actual presence of the risen Jesus in our lives in the twentieth century? Is faith the only way we can know that Jesus continues to be with us, as he promised when he said, "I will be with you always, to the end of the age"?

Four Tugs

I can suggest an answer to this question, but first let me tell you a little story. A small boy and his grandfather were flying a kite. Suddenly the kite disappeared in some low-flying clouds. After five minutes had gone by, the grandfather said to the small boy, "Matthew, how do we know the kite's still up there? Maybe some thief up in those clouds has stolen it." The boy wasn't disturbed by his grandfather's remark. "It's up there, all right, even though we can't see it right now." "But how can you be so sure?" said the grandfather. "I'm not as convinced as you are that it's still up there." "Well," said the small boy, "that's because you don't feel it tug every now and then, as I do."

That story helps me understand something about the way Jesus is present to his followers today. People of faith know Jesus is risen because every now and then they feel him tug. Every now and then they experience the risen presence in their lives.

Nature Experience

How do Christians experience the "tug" of the risen Jesus in their lives? I can identify four kinds of tugs that seem to be experienced universally by many Christians. First of all, there is the tug that they experience in nature itself. In other words, there are things in nature that seem to speak of life after death. There are things in our everyday world that speak of resurrection.

There is a story about a little schoolboy who came to his classroom in tears because of the death of President Kennedy. The little boy cried out, "He's dead, I tell you. He's really dead. The president is dead!"

The teacher wanted to assure the disturbed child that the president wasn't dead in the sense that she feared the child was thinking about death. The teacher put her arm around the child and walked him over to the window. The week before the same child had helped to plant some seeds in a window box in the classroom. The teacher dug into the dirt and located one of the seeds. Lifting the child up, she said, "Look at the seed we planted last week. See, it is brown and soggy and falling apart. But look! Something beautiful is also happening. From the seed a tiny green plant is growing. Something like that is happening to the president right now. His body is dead and in the ground. But something wonderful is also happening to the president, just as something wonderful is happening to this seed.

"God never intended the seed to remain a seed forever. He made it to be something much greater. He made it to be a beautiful plant. It's the same way with us. God never intended us to stay the way we now are. He made us to be something much more beautiful."

Gilbert Chesterton put it this way: "If seeds in the black earth can turn into such beautiful roses, what might the heart of man become in its long journey to the stars?"

In fact the very matter that makes up our star-filled universe gives eloquent testimony to the resurrection. Some of you may remember Wernher von Braun. He is sometimes called the "twentieth-century Columbus." More than any other man, Wernher von Braun is responsible for putting American astronauts on the moon.

Von Braun's career began in Germany. He developed the famed V-2 rocket in World War II. Toward the end of the war, he was also working on the rocket that would reach New York City. As the Russians advanced toward Germany, Von Braun and his staff fled to Bavaria, where they surrendered to the United States.

Within months, Von Braun was at work at White Sands proving grounds in New Mexico. In 1960, he went to work on the rocket system that eventually put our astronauts on the moon.

Before Von Braun died, he made a statement that surprised a lot of people. He said, "Many people seem to feel that science has somehow made 'religious ideas' untimely or old-fashioned. But I think science has a real surprise for the skeptics. Science, for instance, tells us that nothing in nature, not even the tiniest particle, can disappear without a trace. Nature does not know extinction. All it knows is transformation.

"Now, if God applied this fundamental principle to the most minute and insignificant parts of his universe, doesn't it make sense to assume that he applies it also to the human soul? I think it does. And everything science has taught me, and continues to teach me, strengthens my belief in the continuity of our spiritual existence after death. Nothing disappears without a trace. Nature does not know extinction. All it knows is transformation. . . . Nothing disappears without a trace."

That says it all. And so nature itself, from the tiniest seed to the vast solar system, preaches a sermon. It says, "Yes, Jesus is indeed risen, and you, too, are destined to rise as he did."

Heart Experience

The second tug that speaks to Christians of the resurrection is the human heart. Some years ago Peter Berger wrote a book entitled *A Rumor of Angels*. In the book the author spoke of "signals of transcendence." A signal of transcendence is something in this life that points to something beyond this life. Among the signals Berger cites in his book is human hope. Hope is that bold inner voice in you and me that says no to the idea that death is a period at the end of the sentence of life.

In other words, there is something deep down inside us that refuses to say, "This is the end!" In a world where death is the destiny of every living thing, we refuse to concede to death the final victory. We continue to expect a life after death.

This universal experience in the human species, says Berger, is a "signal" that there is indeed something waiting for us after death. In other words, just as there is something that satisfies our hunger for food, our hunger for love, and our hunger for truth, so there is something that satisfies our hunger for eternal life.

There's a memorable scene in Thornton Wilder's Pulitzer prize-winning play, *Our Town*. At the beginning of act three, the stage manager turns to the audience and says, "We all know that *something* is eternal. And it ain't houses, and it ain't names, and it ain't earth, and it ain't even the stars . . . Everybody knows in their bones that *something* is eternal, and that something has to do with human beings.

"There's something way down deep that's eternal about every human being. . . . They're waitin'. They're waitin' for something that they feel is comin'. Something important and great."

Robert Hillyer puts it this way in his book *This I Believe*: "Like many others before me, I have experienced 'intimations of immortality.' I can no more explain these than the brown seed can explain the flowering tree."

And finally, C. S. Lewis says, "If I find in myself a desire which no experience in this world can satisfy, the most probable explanation is that I was made for another world." So the second tug that speaks of the resurrection is the human heart itself.

Experience of Christians

And that brings us to the third tug. It is experienced by those Christians whose faith in Jesus leads to a transformation of their lives. These Christians have risen triumphantly after an experience of spiritual death in their own personal lives.

A striking example of such a person is Joni Eareckson. Many of you are probably familiar with her book entitled *Joni*. It has sold over three million copies and has been made into a motion picture.

One hot afternoon in July, seventeen-year-old Joni suffered a tragic diving accident in the Chesapeake Bay. She was unable to move her arms or her legs. She was rushed to a hospital. There doctors confirmed what everyone feared. Joni was paralyzed from her neck down.

The months following the accident were a nightmare for Joni and her family. The beautiful young athlete who had delighted audiences at horse shows with her riding ability lay strapped to a Stryker frame. Much of the time she lay face down, looking at the floor.

In desperation for something to hang on to, Joni turned, reluctantly at first, to the Bible. Gradually it began to speak to her. She writes, "I'd visualize Jesus standing beside my Stryker . . . saying specifically to me, 'Lo, I am with you always. . . .' I discovered that the Lord Jesus Christ could indeed empathize with my situation. On the cross . . . he was immobilized, helpless."

A remarkable change began to take place in Joni's life. She learned to draw by holding a pen in her teeth. Today she still can't move her arms or legs, yet she is now an acclaimed young artist. She has written two best-sellers, appeared on television shows, and played the lead role in a movie of her own life.

Joni Eareckson is just one of many individuals whose faith in Jesus has led to a transformation in their own lives. She is one of many individuals who have risen victoriously after a tragic experience of spiritual death.

Whenever a person experiences life rising anew from a death situation, that person experiences the resurrection. Whenever you fail and you try again, that's resurrection. Whenever you have your love rejected and you love again, that's resurrection. Whenever you have been betrayed and you trust again, that's resurrection. Each time you pick up the pieces of a broken life and begin again, that's resurrection.

It is a foretaste of the power of the risen Jesus at work in your life. It is a foretaste of the victory of life over death that Jesus experienced on Easter morning. It is a foretaste of the complete triumph of life over death that we will experience on the final day when we, too, are raised from earthly death to eternal life.

Community Experience

A fourth tug that speaks to many Christians of resurrection is the community of the followers of Jesus. We all know what the disciples were like during and after the suffering and death of

Jesus. They were weak. They were afraid and the gospel makes it clear that the disciples were confused about many of the things Jesus taught.

But the resurrection of Jesus and the descent of the Holy Spirit changed all that. Their weakness turned into strength, their fear into courage, and their confusion into understanding.

Completely transformed, the disciples went forth and began to preach the good news: "Jesus had risen!" Their lives were lived for that purpose and for that purpose alone: to tell the world that Jesus was the promised Messiah and that he had risen from the dead.

No amount of persecution could stop them. The disciples were hung on crosses, like Jesus. They were ripped apart by wild beasts in the Roman colosseum. They were burned alive at the stake. But their belief in Jesus never wavered. The lives and sacrifices of these early disciples changed the course of history.

What transformed the disciples from weak men into strong men? What transformed Peter the pile of sand into Peter the rock? What transformed total defeat into total victory? History offers no reason. We have only one explanation. And that is the one the disciples themselves gave: "Jesus had risen from the dead!"

Jesus did more than rise. Through the coming of the Holy Spirit on Pentecost, Jesus united himself with his followers in a remarkable way. The apostle Paul experienced this remarkable unity on the road to Damascus. He learned that to persecute the followers of Jesus was to persecute Jesus.

It was this remarkable unity with Jesus that gave the followers of Jesus their new life and their new power. Paul wrote to the Corinthians:

Christ is like a single body. . . . All of us . . . have been baptized into the one body by the same Spirit.

(1 Corinthians 12:12-13)

And to the Ephesians:

This power working in us is the same as the mighty strength which [God] used when he raised Christ from death and seated him at his right side in the heavenly world. . . . [God] gave [Christ] to the church as supreme Lord over all things. The church is Christ's body, the completion of him who himself completes all things everywhere.

(Ephesians 1:19-23)

And, finally, to the Colossians, Paul writes:

You have been raised to life with Christ. . . . Your real life is Christ and when he appears [at the end of time], then you too will appear with him and share his glory! . . . Christ is all, Christ is in all. You are the people of God; he loved you and chose you for his own.

(Colossians 3:1, 4, 11-12)

As we let your eyes sweep back across the centuries to the first Easter Sunday, we see that the body of Jesus that rose from the tomb was totally different from the body of Jesus that was buried in the tomb. It had made a quantum leap forward into a higher, fuller life.

Because the risen Jesus now lives in a totally different dimension of reality, we can't see him;

we can't hear him; we can't touch him. We can be sure of his presence only by faith. Yet, as we have seen, there are many things in our visible world that speak of resurrection.

Nature itself, from the tiniest seed to the vast solar system, preaches a sermon. It says, "Yes, Jesus is indeed risen; and you, too, are destined to rise as he did."

Remember the story of the child who mourned the president and the conviction of the scientist Wernher von Braun. Our own human heart also speaks of resurrection. Down deep in every person is an unexplainable hunger for a life where there will be no more pain, no more tears, no more death.

C. S. Lewis summed up this hunger, saying, "If I find in myself a desire which no experience in this world can satisfy, the most probable explanation is that I was made for another world."

The transformed and inspired lives of believers speak of resurrection. This shared intuition is a sign of our shared certitude of the resurrection. Whenever we love again after being rejected, hope again after giving up, trust again after having been betrayed, we witness to the power of the risen Jesus helping to raise us from death to life, just as he himself was raised.

Finally, the community of the followers of Jesus is convincing evidence of the resurrection of Jesus.

The Easter experience of the disciples of Jesus changed not only their own personal lives but also the course of world history. No acceptable explanation for this has ever been given, except the one the disciples themselves gave. They have seen Jesus alive. He had kept his promises.

Paul sums up everything this way:

The truth is that Christ has been raised from death, as the guarantee that those who sleep in death will also be raised. For just as death came by means of a man, in the same way the rising from death comes by means of a man. For just as all people die because of their union with Adam, in the same way all will be raised to life because of their union with Christ. . . . Just as we wear the likeness of the man made of earth, so we will wear the likeness of the Man of heaven.

(1 Corinthians 15:20-22, 49)

MEDITATION/DISCUSSION POINTS

1. The book says, "Nature itself, from the tiniest seed to the vast solar system, preaches a sermon. It says, 'Yes, Jesus is indeed risen. . . .'" Review the points it made to illustrate this. Can you think of other examples?

2. In his book *A Rumor of Angels* Peter Berger speaks of "signals of transcendence." Review what he means by these. Reflect on how hope serves as a "signal of transcendence."

3. The book says "Whenever you fail and you try again, that's resurrection. Whenever you have your love rejected and you love again, that's resurrection . . . It is a foretaste of the victory of life over death that Jesus experienced on Easter morning." Recall a time when you tried or loved again.

4. "Whenever you have been betrayed and you trust again, that's resurrection. Each time you pick up the pieces of a broken life and begin again, that's resurrection." Recall a time when you trusted or began again.

5. Which of the four tugs (nature's examples, heart's hunger, transformed individuals, or transformed community) speaks to you most eloquently of Jesus' resurrection to you? Why?